New Studies in the Philosophy of Religion

General Editor: W. D. Hudson, Reader in Moral Philosophy,
University of Exeter

This series of monographs includes studies of all the main
problems in the philosophy of religion. It will be of particular
interest to those who study this subject in universities or
colleges. The philosophical problems connected with religious
belief are not, however, a subject of concern only to specialists;
they arise in one form or another for all intelligent men when
confronted by the appeals or the claims of religion.

The general approach of this series is from the standpoint of
contemporary analytical philosophy, and the monographs are
written by a distinguished team of philosophers, all of whom
now teach, or have recently taught, in British or American
universities. Each author has been commissioned to analyse
some aspect of religious belief; to set forth clearly and concisely
the philosophical problems which arise from it; to take into
account the solutions which classical or contemporary philosophers have offered; and to present his own critical assessment
of how religious belief now stands in the light of these problems
and their proposed solutions.

In the main it is theism with which these monographs deal
because that is the type of religious belief with which readers are
most likely to be familiar, but other forms of religion are not
ignored. Some of the authors are religious believers and some
are not, but it is not their primary aim to write polemically,
much less dogmatically, for or against religion. Rather, they set
themselves to clarify the nature of religious belief in the light of
modern philosophy by bringing into focus the questions about
it which a reasonable man as such has to ask. How is talk of
God like, and how unlike, other universes of discourse in which
men engage, such as science, art or morality? Is this talk of God
self-consistent? Does it accord with other rational beliefs which
we hold about man or the world which he inhabits? It is
questions such as these which this series will help the reader to
answer for himself.

New Studies in the Philosophy of Religion

IN THE SAME SERIES

Published

Religion and Secularisation

VERNON PRATT
Lecturer in Philosophy, University College, Cardiff

Macmillan
St Martin's Press

First published 1970 by
MACMILLAN AND CO LTD
London and Basingstoke
Associated companies in New York Toronto
Dublin Melbourne Johannesburg and Madras

Library of Congress catalog card no. 75-126269

SBN 333 10259 2

Printed in Great Britain by
ROBERT MACLEHOSE AND CO LTD
The University Press, Glasgow

Contents

Editor's Preface

It is sometimes contended that secularisation has rendered religious beliefs meaningless. This view must be clearly distinguished from the once widely held but now largely abandoned opinion that religious beliefs are meaningless simply because they are not, like scientific hypotheses, empirically falsifiable. The secularisation to which I refer is the putative fact that all the presuppositions of our thinking have become atheistic. If, for instance, the roof of his house falls in, the first question which occurs to a modern man is not 'Why has God done this to me?' but something like 'What has gone wrong with the rafters?' The contention is that because a modern man has to depart radically from his normal ways of thinking in order to see any point in religion the latter has become, or is rapidly becoming, meaningless to him.

With secularisation in this sense and its implications Mr Pratt's monograph deals. He attempts to clarify the concept and to assess the extent to which secularisation has in fact occurred. Religious thinkers are of course aware that something of the kind is going on and many of them have attempted to give a 'secular meaning' to religious belief. Mr. Pratt considers a representative selection of such thinkers. Finally he offers his own opinions about what is involved, as he puts it, in living without 'The Beyond'.

Like other monographs in the series 'New Studies in the Philosophy of Religion' the approach is analytical and clarificatory rather than polemical. The author clearly expounds the main thinkers who have contributed to his subject, examines what they say critically, and then adds his own views on the points at issue. His monograph will be of help to the student and of interest to professional philosophers and theologians.

W. D. Hudson

University of Exeter

Preface

I have been helped in writing what follows by my colleagues at Cardiff, and in particular by Robin Attfield; by Ann Taylor and Diana Leat; by my brother Roger Pratt; and, enormously, by Roger Woolhouse. My wife proof-read and was lovely throughout.

If so slight a work can bear the weight of a dedication, I offer it to my parents, who have had the worry of living through some of the issues discussed academically here.

Note: in referring to the writings of others I have said enough in the text to enable full bibliographical details to be looked up in the Bibliography at the end.

University College, Cardiff   Vernon Pratt

1 Losing 'The Beyond'

'The existence of God is not an experimental issue in the way it was.'

John Wisdom

1 Secularisation: The concept and the happening

'Folks don't go to Church anymore': here, it is tempting to think, we have the bedrock of 'secularisation'. Churches stand empty, men to run them fail to come forward, and the talk of those that do is the worried talk of an enclave under siege. If secularisation can be identified with the waning of institutional religion, then Britain can be shown by reference to readily available figures (e.g. Wilson, ch. 1) to be secularising steadily.

But if we say we live in a secular society we refer, I think, not only to the fact that people don't go to church, but also to their occupations while so absenting themselves. We have in mind, that is to say, a distinctive way of life. What are its characteristics?

(a) Some marks of a secular society

Harvey Cox attempts an answer in his study of 'The Secular City'.

One feature he regards as important is what he calls the 'anonymity' of modern life. A great many of the relationships with which a modern urban dweller has to be involved are in a sense 'impersonal'. When we visit a bank, for example, we do not expect to be drawn into a discussion of the clerk's 'private affairs'. He is to us not Walter Perkins, married with five kids, worried about the mortgage, thinking of his roses and dreading the week-end when his sister-in-law is coming to stay: but a bank clerk, a man whose job as far as we are concerned is to count out our money and hand it over with efficiency and courteousness. Because the urban dweller relies on a highly complex 'net of services to maintain himself in existence' (of which the bank is just one example) this kind of relationship is typical: 'the majority of his transactions will have to be public and will be what sociologists call functional or secondary. ... Urban life demands that we treat most of the people we meet

1

as persons – not as things, but not as intimates either. This in turn produces [a] kind of 'immunisation' against personal encounters [which] results in a way of life which often appears cold and even heartless to those unfamiliar with the dynamics of urban living' (Cox, pp. 41–2).

Secondly, Cox stresses the mobility of modern life, and as in the first case he is of course only repeating a commonplace of social criticism. People move house easily and frequently in pursuit of jobs or improvement; and even when their base remains fixed, they very often 'commute' – not only to work 'but also to play, to shop, to socialise' (Cox, p. 50).

Cox believes, I take it (Cox, pp. 4–5), that secularisation and urbanisation are connected in a *factual* (as opposed to a conceptual) way, and so it seems that the two characteristics mentioned so far are best regarded in Cox's scheme as marks of urban rather than secular society proper. When he goes on to pick out other characteristics, however, he seems to be discussing the marks of the secular society as such. He lays great stress on what he calls *pragmatism* and *profanity*, which he explains as follows:

> By *pragmatism* we mean secular man's concern with the question 'Will it work?' Secular man does not occupy himself much with mysteries. He is little interested in anything that seems resistant to the application of human energy and intelligence. He judges ideas . . . by the results they will achieve in practice. The world is viewed not as a unified metaphysical system but as a series of problems and projects.
>
> By *profanity* we refer to secular man's wholly terrestrial horizon, the disappearance of any supramundane reality. . . . He views the world not in terms of some other world but in terms of itself. (Cox, pp. 60–1)

With the profanity of secular society, as Cox has defined it, we shall be much concerned in what follows; and his notion of *pragmatism* we shall discuss further as it reappears in another writer. Let us note meanwhile that two further characteristics of a secular society in Cox's view are *pluralism* and *tolerance* (Cox, pp. 2–3). In secular society, he thinks, different 'world-views', including different 'religions', peacefully coexist without the fanaticism which has been so disruptive in the past.

Cox therefore agrees that 'religion', or what has the appear-

2

ance of religion, can survive secularisation. But in this case, he argues, it becomes a mere hobby, 'a mark of national or ethnic identification', or, it may be, 'an esthetic delight'. No longer does it provide for the bulk of people 'an inclusive and commanding system of personal values and explanations'.

Cox goes on to develop the major thesis of his book, which is the interesting and ingeniously argued view that a 'secular' society – a society characterised by 'pluralism', 'tolerance', 'pragmatism' and 'profanity', as well as the 'mobility' and 'anonymity' arising from its being urban – need not be non-Christian. Properly understood, Cox argues, Christianity's conception of the ideal way of life necessarily involves a *secular* form of society in the sense explained. This unfortunately is a question which we cannot take further, except that a later discussion of whether Christianity is *compatible* with 'profanity' will clearly have some bearing.

Bryan Wilson has written about *Religion in Secular Society*, though without, as far as I can see, facing head on the question of what distinguishes a secular society from a non-secular one. In passing, however, he makes observations which support some of Cox's suggestions, as well as adding to them. In discussing American society, Wilson mentions three features which mark it out as secular: the prevalence there of instrumental values, of rational procedures and of technical methods, and he adds that a secular society is one where 'the sense of the sacred, the sense of the sanctity of life, and deep religiosity are . . . absent' (Wilson, p. 112).

These suggestions as to what characterises secular society together with those of Cox do no more than expand on the familiar form of definition of secularisation as 'the process whereby religious thinking, practice and institutions lose social significance' (Wilson, p. 14). They specify what is the effect in each particular aspect of life when its religious orientation is lost. For example, when men without religion want to get something done they turn to science, not to prayer: their methods are what Wilson calls 'technical'. Again, since religious beliefs are typically matters of great conviction – they are, as we shall hear D. Z. Phillips saying later, 'absolutes' for the believers themselves – a society which is monolithic and intolerant when it is religious tends (I mean this as a matter of *fact*, not of logical connection) to become pluralistic and tolerant as it secularises.

3

Two of Wilson's suggestions, however, seem to me to need clarification. First the phrase 'rational procedures' is open, I think, to misunderstanding. It is the same notion that appears in the title of Lecky's book 'The Rise and Influence of Rationalism in Europe', where the progress which we are calling 'secularisation' is so well charted. But the implication of this way of talking – that a religious society is non-rational – is apt to be very misleading. The difference between a secular society and a religious one is that different sorts of things *count* as reasons in the two contexts, not that reasons are given in one but not in the other. In medieval society, for example, an appeal in the course of debate to an 'authority' would be regarded as a perfectly 'rational' procedure; but in our contemporary context citing someone else's opinion would not (*in itself*, of course) count as providing a reason at all. (And one can readily see *why* it was reasonable to appeal to tradition, when belief in divine revelation safeguarded by a divinely instituted Church was a basic and undoubted article of faith.)

Second, Wilson's reference to 'instrumental values' is not perfectly clear. I take it that he means by the phrase something similar to Cox's notion of 'pragmatism'. Secular man, asserts Cox, 'is interested in what will work to get something done' (Cox, p. 62). He is concerned with the question 'Will it work?' (Cox, p. 60).

This could be taken to mean that the question of what we *want* done, the question of what it is a man wants doing when he asks whether such and such 'will work', the question of ends as contrasted with means, simply does not arise for secular man. But if this is so, as it may be, it is because there is *general agreement* over ends, and not because ends no longer enter into the question. Questions about what ought to be done become questions of what means are the most efficient only if we are agreed as to ends. 'Pragmatism' is possible as a moral philosophy only where there is consensus.

The difference between secular and religious systems of values, it is therefore suggested, is not that the one refers to ends while the other doesn't, but that the ends involved in the two cases are different. In a typically religious society many things are done in order to achieve 'supernatural' objects – 'eternal life', it may be – objects which are clearly not possible for secular man.

The waning of religious institutions then, though perhaps the
4

most obvious, is not the only mark of a secularising society. Others, as we have seen, have been suggested by Cox and Wilson: tolerance and pluralism, the dominance of 'instrumental' values, 'rational' procedures and 'technical' methods, an absence of 'the sense of the sacred', and a general orientation of thinking called by Cox 'profanity'.

It is of course true that none of the characteristics mentioned, and none that could be mentioned, are common to *all* secular societies; nor are any *peculiar* to them. It seems right to regard the United States as a secular society in spite of the fact that its religious institutions are going from strength to strength (see Wilson, ch. 6), and for a long while Indian society was pluralistic without being secular. All that is claimed is that the characteristics mentioned are *typical* of secularised societies.

David Martin has made so much of a meal out of the absence of features that are common and peculiar to secular societies that he has succumbed to indigestion as a result, and he is to be found pronouncing somewhat sourly that the very concept of secularisation should be dispensed with. His argument, however (to be found in his article 'Towards Eliminating the Concept of Secularisation'), is based on the tempting but highly dubious thesis that for every sort of thing there is a feature (or set of features) which is possessed by everything of that sort but not by anything else, and that it is the possession of such a feature (or set of features) which justifies us in subsuming the thing under a particular general term. (We might call this the 'common and peculiar features' view.)

But alternative theories about the application of general terms have been canvassed, notably the 'family resemblance' view which Wittgenstein adumbrated in 'Philosophical Investigations (§ 65 ff.). Later (pp. 57 ff.) I shall say something more about this issue (though not much). For the present we may simply note the possibility of such an alternative, so as not to feel too inadequate in characterising a secular society in terms of what is *typical* of such: we need not feel, I suggest, as Martin does, the absolute necessity to set down common and peculiar characteristics.

(b) Two aspects of secularisation
Our list of features which have been claimed as typical of

secular society indicate that we have to distinguish two aspects of secularisation: it can be regarded in the first place as a *social* process, and in the second as an *intellectual* one.

The waning of religious institutions is most obviously seen as a social change. To a considerable extent it can be measured unproblematically – by counting Church membership, recruits to the Ministry (or equivalent), numbers of new buildings erected, and so forth. We are dealing, that is to say, with the fortunes of a social institution (or institutions) which lend themselves readily to relatively straightforward empirical study.

But if we take Cox's notion of 'profanity' the case is very different. Cox is using this term to apply not to a social institution but to a general orientation of mind. 'By *profanity*', he says, 'we refer to secular man's wholly terrestrial horizon, the disappearance of any supramundane reality defining his life' (Cox, p. 60). Cox is saying that we no longer think in terms of 'the Supernatural'. Our world-view has changed, our conceptual framework altered.

Paul van Buren makes the same kind of remark when rightly or not he claims concerning 'God' that as members of a secular society 'we no longer know how to use the word at all' ('The Secular Meaning of the Gospel, p. 191).

These assertions are about *concepts* – about the plausibility and validity of arguments, about intelligibility. They speak of an (alleged) *intellectual* development. They make claims which fall within the aegis of the history of ideas.

Part of the intellectual change that Cox and van Buren are referring to shows itself well in a comment about Henry Sidgwick, made by J. M. Keynes and quoted by Alasdair MacIntyre. Keynes is puzzled as to how it was possible for a clever, percipient man like Sidgwick to spend so much time worrying about the truth of a doctrine – Christianity – which was so clearly false:

Have you ever read Sidgwick's Life? Very interesting and depressing. He never did anything but wonder whether Christianity was true, and prove that it wasn't, and hope that it was. Oh, I suppose he was intimate but he didn't seem to have anything to be intimate about exactly, except his religious doubts, and he really ought to have got over that a

6

little sooner, because he knew that the thing wasn't true perfectly well from the beginning.

('Secularisation and Moral Change', p. 37)

About half a century separates these two men; and in that time the 'intellectual climate', if that is the appropriate phrase, has altered, to the extent that of two equally intelligent, sensitive people one can find it necessary to devote immense intellectual and emotional energy to the question of Christianity's truth, while another finds it *obviously* false.

Norman Kemp Smith begins his essay 'Is Divine Existence Credible?' by remarking the same phenomenon. Many people nowadays, he notes, assume as a matter of course that 'belief in God is no longer possible for any really enlightened mind' (Smith, p. 105); and he quotes a document produced by a recent Lambeth Conference which confesses that 'We [the Archbishops and Bishops in session] are aware of the extent to which the very thought of God seems to be passing away from the minds and hearts of many even in nominally Christian nations' (Smith, p. 105). Things have not always been so, says Professor Smith. In David Hume's time, for example, the question of God's existence was at least a matter of lively discussion; and so the question arises: 'Why is it that what was, at the least, an open question for David Hume, is for many no longer worthy even of debate?' (Smith, p. 105).

Widening the time scale even further, we have as a contrast with our own situation of widespread scepticism the universal belief of the Middle Ages. As MacIntyre baldly puts it: 'Up to the seventeenth century we should in our society all have been believers and indeed there would be no question of our being anything else' ('Is Understanding Religion Compatible with Believing?', p. 128).

In that situation what has been called 'The Christian Mind' could flourish; and we take our final illustration of the intellectual aspect of secularisation from a man who uses this phrase as the title of his book. 'A prime mark of the Christian mind', we read, 'is that it cultivates the eternal perspective. That is to say, it looks beyond this life to another one. It is supernaturally oriented, and brings to bear upon earthly considerations the fact of Heaven and the fact of Hell' (Harry Blamires, 'The Christian Mind', p. 67).

7

Though flourishing once, such a mind, it is asserted, no longer exists, even among those who remain, in a sense, 'Christian'. The writer addresses himself to his fellow believers: 'Do we', he asks, 'mentally inhabit a world . . . in which man is called to live daily, hourly, in contact with the God whom neither time nor space can limit? Do we, as Christians, mentally inhabit an order of being which is superior to decay and death? . . . The truth is that for the most part we don't (Blamires, p. 76).

There was a time when belief in God was universal; but since then atheism or agnosticism has passed from being the faith of a tiny and harassed minority and become a respectable credo – even, almost, an orthodoxy; while in the last few years any position which uses the word 'God', if only to question or deny his existence, has been attacked from the theological left as old-fashioned on the grounds that the term is simply meaningless.

The relationship between this intellectual development and what I have called the social aspect of secularisation, of which the decline in public support of the religious institutions is the most obvious and manipulable mark, does not at first sight seem at all problematic. To take the extreme case, what could be more natural than that people who no longer understand what the word 'God' means should desist from going to Church? Or, what else is to be expected but that people who lack the concept of the supernatural should omit to call on its help when they want to get something done?

To this *simpliste* view of the nature of the relationship between the two aspects of secularisation I have no wish to commit myself. More than one large objection weighs against it. For example, when we investigate the self-confessed beliefs of those who choose to have little to do with institutional religion, we do not find the universal scepticism the above view would lead us to expect. Geoffrey Gorer's survey of 1955, for example, led him to conclude that about a quarter of the population, which must include a good number of those who neglect the institutions of religion, hold 'a view of the universe which can most properly be designated as magical' ('Exploring English Character', p. 269), and the widespread appeal of superstition among the (largely non-church- or chapel-going) working class has been noted by several writers (see MacIntyre, 'Secularisation and

Moral Change', p. 17; Hoggart, 'Uses of Literacy', pp. 29, 30).
If I am right in thinking that superstitious beliefs and religious
beliefs share the concept of the supernatural, then facts like
these mean that we cannot appeal to the loss of the concept in
order to explain why people no longer go to church (or
equivalent): too often they appear to embrace the concept but
not the institution.

The relation between the two aspects of secularisation I take,
then, to be not at all easy to analyse; but I do think one can see
clearly enough to regard as highly paradoxical any account of
secularisation which regards the two aspects as *independent*: yet
such a view I seem to discern in the stimulating and impressive
little book by MacIntyre we have already referred to: 'Secularisation and Moral Change'. To a criticism of some of the points
MacIntyre makes there I now turn.

S KIP

(c) An anti-intellectualist account of secularisation
MacIntyre declares in his introduction that he is going to mean
by 'secularisation' 'simply the transition from beliefs and activities and institutions presupposing beliefs of a traditional
Christian kind to beliefs and activities and institutions of an
atheistic kind' (MacIntyre, [1] pp. 7–8).

Very curiously, on the sole grounds presumably that its religious institutions are flourishing, MacIntyre holds (MacIntyre,
[1] p. 34) that American society is *not* secularised; though to
take the view that modern American society exhibits beliefs
and institutions and activities presupposing beliefs 'of a traditional Christian kind' seems, prima facie, strange, to say the
least.

The point of immediate interest to us however arises when
MacIntyre's definition is placed alongside one of the chief theses
of his book, which is that the roots of the secularisation of
English society are to be found in the Industrial Revolution:
'. . . the explanation both of the secularisation of English society
and of the limits to that secularisation are to be found in the
changes in the value-system of the community, brought about
by the Industrial Revolution and by the consequent class
division of English society' (MacIntyre, [1] p. 58).

Against this, I want to argue the view that secularisation,
even as MacIntyre has defined it, was well underway *before*

industrialisation, and that the movement to the towns merely added fuel to a fire that was already burning.

It is of course difficult to know exactly what count as 'beliefs . . . of a traditional Christian kind'. Would the medieval belief in Hell qualify? – that is, belief in a Hell which imposed literally physical tortures on the damned, and in which they were subject to *literal* flames? It certainly figured largely in the Christianity of the time: indeed its role was a dominating one. Yet it came to be rejected, and by a process which had begun by the time of the Industrial Revolution. Lecky puts Descartes at the beginning of this process, and its last controversy in the first half of the eighteenth century (The Rise and Influence of 'Rationalism in Europe', i 344–51).

Belief in witchcraft similarly was undeniably on the decline by the time Joseph Glanvill published the first version of his celebrated defence of it, 'Sadducismus Triumphatus', in 1666 (see Willey, 'The Seventeenth Century Background', p. 194, first footnote); and yet no one can doubt the importance of this belief to English Christianity at the time of the Reformation, and particularly under 'the gloomy theology of the Puritans'. (Lecky's phrase, i 108; and see Lecky in general on this topic, i 108 ff.)

Religious intolerance, too, resting on the Christian belief in the eternal damnation of all who did not belong to the Church (the doctrine which 'has had a greater influence than perhaps any other speculative opinion upon the history of mankind' in Lecky's view (i 378)), had come under serious challenge well before the end of the seventeenth century (Lecky, ii 70 ff.).

My point is simply that if MacIntyre sticks by his definition of 'secularisation' as including a reference to traditional Christian beliefs, as, broadly, I think he would be right to do, then it is a process which is much more plausibly identified with the changes associated with the Reformation and Scientific Renaissance than it is with those initiated by the Industrial Revolution.

Incidentally MacIntyre himself passes on, but fails to heed, a hint that the beginning of secularisation cannot be identified with urbanisation when he argues (MacIntyre, [1] p. 11) on statistical grounds that *before* the mass of people moved from the countryside many town-dwellers must have been non-church-goers: this shows, surely, that secularisation, even in its social aspect, had already begun.)

10

If then it is granted – and I do not see how it can be denied – that the intellectual process which I have claimed to be one aspect of secularisation was underway before the massive move to the towns took place, then either MacIntyre is wrong in regarding the latter as inaugurating secularisation, or he is involved in maintaining that this intellectual process is not an aspect of secularisation at all.

But this second alternative is too paradoxical to accept. For consider: over the last three centuries you have on the one hand a gradual change from a situation in which there was tacit agreement that God's existence was unquestionable, to the situation as it is today – in which his existence is doubted by many, denied by many and regarded by others as a meaningless issue; while on the other hand you have a transition from almost total support of those very social structures which give institutional form to belief in God, to almost total neglect of them. Is it not incredible that two developments, so intimately connected 'on the level of meaning', as the sociologist might say, should be independent of each other? It *is* incredible: MacIntyre must be wrong.

In my view, it is clear that industrialisation, of which urbanisation is an aspect, was dependent on the *intellectual* development that comprised the origins of modern science; and in my view too it is in the conceptual changes wrought by the same scientific revolution that we should look for the elucidation of the intellectual aspect of secularisation. Neither of these views imply, or should be taken to imply, that the beginnings of modern science were not themselves rooted in changes in the social and economic structure of medieval society: but this is a question we cannot pursue.

Instead, we turn all our attention now on the intellectual aspect of secularisation, having said perhaps a necessary word in its defence. PICK UP

2 Secularisation of the mind

I have said that the origins of the intellectual aspect of secularisation are to be found in the scientific revolution of the seventeenth century. My argument will be that the development of science has given rise to a conceptual framework importantly different from that in which 'traditional Christianity' flourished.

11

In particular, I believe that the scientific conceptual framework with which we are living today has no place for the concept of the supernatural, and it is this circumstance which the 'secularisers' of Christianity – that is, those Christians who are attempting to preserve their religion in the face of secularisation – are feeling it necessary to face. They are attempting to 'de-supernaturalise' a 'supernatural' religion, because the notion of the supernatural no longer has any meaning.

I realise that I am involved here in the paradoxical but immensely popular procedure of philosophers who understand a notion quite well enough to argue its unintelligibility. As I have heard Professor Geach put it in his inimitable way, one of the ancients argued compellingly that certain notions of his opponent's were so much birdsong, without explaining why he found it necessary to argue with the latter but not with the birds.

In a sense it is undeniable that people 'know what is meant' by terms like 'the Supernatural', or 'God'. They know what an angel is. They can answer questions about Heaven and Hell. They know what is meant by a 'miracle'. When Geoffrey Gorer asked about these things he did not meet blankly uncomprehending faces. He met those who believed in their reality and those who did not, but the question of *whether* they believed in them seemed to be received as perfectly intelligible (Gorer, ch. 14).

But could they – can anyone – give a *coherent account* of what is meant by these notions? Could we explain their meaning without involving ourselves in contradictions, or without relying on distinctions which in fact cannot be maintained? Would we have to resort before our account was done to irreducible metaphors or to irremovable quotation marks? Here is one account, for example, so overcrusted with devices such as these that it is likely to go down without a trace:

By 'the supernatural', in contrast, I shall mean the whole body of thought and activity which is concerned with man's life as a member of 'another world', which sees his life in 'this world' as deriving ultimately from that 'other world' and which sees his final destiny as lying in that 'other world' and beyond bodily death.

(E. L. Mascall, 'The Secularisation of Christianity', p. 191)

12

Basically, my claim is that although people often think they know what these notions mean, no coherent account can in the end be given of them.

(a) *The naturalisation of 'the Supernatural'*

How then has the concept of the supernatural been banished by science? What is the basis for our claim that a scientific world-view and belief in 'the Supernatural' are incompatible?

Some have suggested that the incompatibility resided in the fact that the world of strict and universal laws which, as it were, science was discovering as it began its modern development in the seventeenth century had no place for the capricious inter-ference of 'supernatural' beings. The world began to be seen not as the haunting-pitch of alien spirits, but as a system of com-ponents working together in obedience to the ineluctable laws of mechanics. It is true that this new conception did not at first seem incompatible with the notion of God – indeed, as Willey tells us, 'it was felt [in the early days of the scientific revolution] that science had produced a conclusive demonstration of God, by showing the evidence of His wisdom and power in the Creation' ('The Touch of Cold Philosophy', p. 374). Neverthe-less, although God was still thought of, he was thought of in a way that differed from the medieval: not as likely to interfere in the everyday running of the universe, but as the remote and magnificent Cause of a machine quite well enough contrived to operate indefinitely on its own.

This approach, then, stresses that science looks upon nature as subject to universal and ineluctable laws: 'supernatural' events are discredited because they are by their very nature supposed to be disruptions of the natural order.

A closely similar suggestion is that science declares that nothing can happen unless it has a natural cause, and that supernatural events – events which at least lack natural causes – are therefore not possible.

Both suggestions (and they are almost identical) are making, I think, a *methodological* point: that 'supernatural' phenomena were discredited not because of science's findings but because its methods ruled them out.

In general terms it seems clear that where the appeal of old had been to the pronouncements of authority, science insisted

13

on referring to observation, experiment and 'reason'. As Basil Willey declares, a major fruit of the scientific revolution was 'a distrust of all tradition, a determination to accept nothing as true merely on authority, but only after experiment and verification' ('The Touch of Cold Philosophy' pp. 373–4).

Thus, to be accepted as authentic, it became no longer enough for an alleged miracle to have been recorded by one of the Fathers: it had to pass the new tests of science.

As far as mature science is concerned, I think it is clear that the crucial test regarding 'supernatural' phenomena was the requirement that for evidence to be scientifically acceptable it had to be *reproducible*. Science demands, in other words, that before a phenomenon can be regarded as having really occurred, it has to be satisfied that if the conditions in which it occurred were to be repeated, the phenomenon itself would also recur. The modern experimenter, for example, is required, in reporting his results, to describe his apparatus and procedure in detail sufficient to enable his results to be checked by any interested parties. If they then fail to obtain the same results his original report is discredited.

This 'reproducibility' criterion is at the very heart of science (but see later pp. 15 ff): to insist on it is simply to insist on the very principle of (natural) causality – the principle that 'like conditions produce like effects'. David Bohm puts it in this way: '. . . we [scientists] do not admit the possibility of arbitrary variations of an effect that are totally unrelated to variations in the state of things from which the effect came' ('Causality and Chance in Modern Physics', p. 8).

Why do 'supernatural' phenomena necessarily fail the 'reproducibility' criterion? Or, what we have said amounts to the same question, why do they necessarily offend the principle of causality? The answer is that if they did *not*, we could not distinguish them from 'non-supernatural' events. For if they *were* reproducible, we should be at least well on the way to providing them with an explanation. As Professor Flew argues, once you have established that there are 'reliable regularities' between a phenomenon's occurrence and the conditions in which it occurs, you have the basis of a 'causal law' ('Hume's Philosophy of Belief', ch. 4), and so the phenomenon becomes 'explicable'.

Science, then, really loads the dice against 'supernatural'
14

events. To accept them as events at all, it demands that they should be reproducible; but any reproducible phenomenon is in principle scientifically explicable and so not 'supernatural'.

Our thesis that it is science's methodology which is responsible for its incompatibility with 'supernatural' phenomena is, as we have pointed out, in no conflict with the suggestion that it is due to science's insistence that every event has a natural cause. Nor is it in conflict with the first-mentioned suggestion that the incompatibility is a result of science's insistence on a 'universal rule of law'. For the reproducibility criterion is a way of ruling out the possibility of events which do not happen according to determinate laws.

That then is my account of how 'supernatural' phenomena came to be eliminated as modern science became established, with the result that by the beginning of the twentieth century certainly the great bulk of what had once been regarded as 'manifestations of spiritual agency' (I take the phrase from an extraordinary and antique work by William Howitt called 'The History of the Supernatural') had become to most thinkers scientifically disreputable. The demise of witchcraft carried away with it a number of 'supernatural' activities – intercourse with devils, devil-possession, levitation, sorcery, foreknowledge and some more; while the other great triumph of science was over the *miraculous*, first in discrediting the exotic profusion of medieval miracle-working, and later in mounting a pretty successful though not wholly conclusive attack on the biblical miracles themselves. All these, once the earthly signs of 'supernatural' society, both nefarious and divine, came to be regarded as intellectually discredited.

There is one consideration which I must at least mention before this discussion of the elimination of 'supernatural' phenomena can be allowed to close. I have based my remarks on the tenet that what I have called 'the reproducibility criterion' of scientific evidence, and the principle of causality which I have identified with it are absolutely basic to the methods of science. Yet since the early years of the twentieth century many scientists have been prepared to recognise events which 'have no cause', and by the same token events which do not happen according to determinate laws (see e.g. E. Nagel, 'The Structure of Science', pp. 293–316). If our account of the elimination of 'the Supernatural' is to be acceptable, does there not have to be a good reason why the rejection or at least the modification of the reproducibility criterion and the associated principle of causality which these developments seem to imply did not lead to the rehabilitation of 'supernatural' phenomena?

This problem I mention because it *has* to be mentioned, not because I know what to say about it. But we may note at least that some qualified thinkers seem to accept what we have said brazenly above, that the principle of causality is utterly basic to science, and that those who try to discard it know not what they do. We may also note that in fact by the time of the advent of these highly perplexing developments 'supernatural' phenomena had been effectively eliminated; and it may just be that the Enlightenment view of the universe as a perfect piece of mechanical engineering had made the idea of particular 'supernatural' interference so unthinkable that when the Great Machine fell apart, unthinkable it remained.

One effect of the new indeterminate physics may be to cast doubt on the easy identification we have made between the principle of causality and that of reproducibility: for in a sense the 'reproducibility' criterion as I have described it (pp. 14 f.) still seems to be universally applied, with the difference that results are typically expressible only in statistical form. It is interesting to note, I think, that the use of the reproducibility criterion in science has allowed the survival of a bogus concept of the supernatural, an account of which may do something to substantiate my earlier claim (pp. 12/f.) that it is possible for someone to think they understand what can be shown to be an incoherent notion.

Confusion arises because alongside the criterion which science uses to distinguish valid from invalid claims – reproducibility – there exists a different criterion, or set of criteria, which we use when we have hung up our white coats and are engaged on our ordinary everyday activities.

For then we regard as highly important such things as the number of witnesses of the alleged event, their integrity, an examination of circumstances with regard to the possibility of fraud, and so on. In other words, in making up our minds as to what has happened, we use in ordinary life a 'criterion (or set of criteria) of validity' quite different from that of science, on the basis of which we are prepared to acknowledge that an event occurred *even though* it may be non-reproducible. There

16

thus arises a class of alleged events which, because they are unreproducible, science regards as bogus, but which by our everyday criteria are judged as authentic: ghosts, poltergeists, table-tappings, telepathic communications and so on. Examples in abundance are to be found in the anthology compiled by Myers, Gurney and Podmore, 'Phantasms of the Living', or in Howitt's 'History of the Supernatural'. Alleged events purportedly described in such works remain 'scientifically inexplicable' not so much because science *cannot* explain them but rather because, regarding them as bogus, it *sees no need* to explain them. What we take to be a fact, science continues to declare an impossibility.

And so a kind of bogus 'Supernatural' remains – a weed, as it were, eking out an existence on the strip of waste ground between the scientific and 'everyday' criteria of validity.

The problems raised, however, for my account by indeterminate physics remain. Without feeling able to say anything more in this context about them, let me at least illustrate the fact that 'supernatural' phenomena *have been* discredited and remain so. This I do by comparing some remarks of Henry Sidgwick's, written almost at the inauguration of the Society for Psychical Research (which set out to study those alleged 'supernatural' phenomena which had survived into the nineteenth century), with something written by C. D. Broad in 1962.

Sidgwick says: '*In the end* if the S.P.R.'s work [Society for Psychical Research] should all be negative, it will be regarded by sceptics as the last element of proof necessary to complete the case against Christianity and other historical religions' (quoted by C. D. Broad, 'Religion, Philosophy and Psychical Research', p. 96).

This indicates that the alleged phenomena to be studied were still being thought of in the 1860s as evidence of a 'supernatural' reality, the 'other-worldly' reality of which Christianity has traditionally spoken.

The point of interest is that the work of the society has *not* been all negative. Yet does that fact count in any way whatever against the religious sceptic's case today? Surely not.

For look at Broad's conclusions. He insists that a small but irreducible number of cases investigated by the society have emerged unscathed and that especially in view of the evidence

17

provided by experimental studies (for a very useful recent guide to these, see John Beloff's appendix to J. R. Smythies, 'Science and E.S.P.') the occurrence of at least certain types of what have traditionally been alleged to be 'supernatural' phenomena must be accepted. But the kind of theory that he adumbrates by way of suggesting what might be required to cover the established evidence makes it clear that he does not regard them as '*supernatural*' phenomena: they do not manifest to his twentieth-century eyes a 'supernatural reality', a 'world beyond'; they simply argue a greater complexity of *this* world. For example, his suggestion as to what might have to be envisaged in order to take account of certain mediumistic phenomena is that there is in the human being a 'ψ-component', which can be thought of as '. . . analogous to a persistent vortex in the ether, carrying modulations imposed on it by experiences had by the person with whose physical body it was formerly associated as a kind of "field" '. He goes on: 'Then we can conceive the possibility of partial coalescence, partial mutual annulment or reinforcement, interference, etc., between the ψ-components of several deceased human beings, in conjunction perhaps with non-human psychic flotsam and jetsam which may exist around us' ('Lectures on Psychical Research', p. 430). Though certainly bizarre, there is, I suggest, no element of 'the *Supernatural*' in this account. In other words, Broad has accepted the occurrence of what were traditionally regarded as 'supernatural phenomena', but has recategorised them as bespeaking not another world, but a greater complexity in this one.

(b) The force of verificationism

But how does this discussion of 'supernatural phenomena' bear upon the concept of *God*? My strategy has been to bring out the reasons why theology has weathered so badly the verificationist storms of the thirties of this century and after. For the result of the elimination of 'supernatural' phenomena has been to rob all 'supernatural' terms of their empirical implications. It has been to effect a radical separation between this world and the 'supernatural' world, such that the latter never shows itself in the former.

But we have to ask: Is this conception of a radically separate world conceptually coherent? What sense is there in talking of something which makes no difference whatever to our experience – which carries no empirical implications? What point can there be in asserting the existence of a 'supernatural world' if its existence makes no difference to the world of our experience?

The point here is the very familiar one wielded to such effect by the logical positivists. In his beautiful 'Language, Truth and Logic' A. J. Ayer, at that time their chief representative in this country, wrote as follows:

What is not . . . generally recognised is that there can be no way of proving that the existence of a god, such as the God of Christianity, is even probable. Yet this is easily shown. For if the existence of such a god were probable, then the proposition that he existed would be an empirical hypothesis. And in that case it would be possible to deduce from it, and other empirical hypotheses, certain experiential propositions which were not deducible from those other hypotheses alone. But in fact this is not possible. (Ayer, p. 115)

Our point comes across even better in terms of John Wisdom's parable of the garden, so well known now that were it not for its precise relevance we could hardly be excused for quoting it:

Two people return to their long neglected garden and find among the weeds a few of the old plants surprisingly vigorous. One says to the other 'It must be that a gardener has been coming and doing something about these plants'. Upon enquiry they find that no neighbour has ever seen anyone at work in their garden. The first man says to the other 'He must have worked while people slept'. The other says 'No, someone would have heard him and besides, anybody who cared about the plants would have kept down these weeds'. The first man says 'Look at the way these are arranged. There is purpose and a feeling for beauty here. I believe that someone comes, someone invisible to mortal eyes. I believe that the more carefully we look the more we shall find confirmation of this.' They examine the garden ever so carefully and sometimes they come on new things suggesting that a gardener comes and sometimes they come on new things suggesting the contrary and even that a malicious person has been at work. Besides examining the garden carefully they also study what happens to gardens left without attention. Each learns all the other learns about this and about the garden. Consequently, when after all this, one says 'I still believe a gardener comes' while the other says 'I don't' their different words now reflect no difference as to what they have found in the garden, no difference as to what they would find in the garden if they looked further and no difference about how fast untended gardens fall into disorder. At this stage, in this context, the gardener hypothesis has ceased to be experimental. . . . (Wisdom, 'Gods', § 6.1)

What sense is there in the first man's insisting that he still believes that a gardener comes? Granted that the gardener's existence has no implications for experience – for what we see, hear, smell, feel and so on – then what *sense* is there in saying that he exists? Surely, there is none.

This may or may not be the moral Wisdom himself derives from the story; but it is the one that seems justified to me. Antony Flew agrees. He has the Sceptic crying, at the conclusion of a slightly modified version of this parable, which Flew presents in 'Theology and Falsification': 'But what remains of your original assertion? Just how does what you call an invisible, intangible, eternally elusive gardener differ from an imaginary gardener or even from no gardener at all?' ('New Essays in Philosophical Theology', ed. Flew and MacIntyre, p. 96).

Our thesis (and that is a pompous name for so familiar a view) is thus that science eliminated 'supernatural' phenomena because of a basic incompatibility of presupposition, and that without any implications for man's experience, all talk involving 'the Supernatural' has become in consequence meaningless.

(c) An alternative account of intellectual secularisation
For a partially different view of how the intellectual aspect of secularisation is to be understood, we turn now to some further writing of Alasdair MacIntyre.

In his paper 'Is Understanding Religion Compatible with Believing?' MacIntyre addresses himself to our basic question.
20

How is it, he asks, that 'one group of men in the past found Christian beliefs obviously true and intelligible and another group now find them opaque[?]' (MacIntyre, [2] p. 128).

MacIntyre suggests two reasons. One is that part at least of the point of Christian concepts lies in their bearing upon behaviour; and that changes in patterns of behaviour since medieval times have deprived those concepts of point: such a concept 'can no longer be embodied in life as it once was, and it is either put to new uses or it becomes redundant'. A non-religious example of this kind of change would be, says MacIntyre, 'the concept of honour detached from the institutions of chivalry' (MacIntyre, [2] p. 127).

When he comes to explain what his thesis amounts to as far as religious concepts are concerned, I think he runs together two distinct points (which are nevertheless not incompatible). One is that the moral principles which Christianity lays down are not, in today's society, *distinctive* – they are recognised by Christian and non-Christian alike. The other is that religious practices do not produce 'higher standards of behaviour' – as judged, presumably, on consensus criteria.

Neither point, it seems to me, helps in the least to explain why Christianity seemed obviously true in the Middle Ages, and yet obviously problematical today – which is the question at issue. For there was nothing *distinctive* about Christian moral principles in medieval times: they were the only ones available. And for much the same reason, there was nothing distinctive about Christian moral achievement: no comparison with non-Christian moral achievement could be made.

Even if one were to accept MacIntyre's two points, therefore, they seem unable to provide the explanation required. So to go on to question one of them is unnecessary, though irresistible.

Is it true then that there is in today's society nothing distinctive about Christian moral principles? Reflection only enlivens my astonishment that this should seriously be asserted. I suppose it depends on what you take to be Christian moral principles; but even identifying them with those urged upon us from unexceptional Anglican pulpits, the remarkable thing is not that they are indistinguishable from the principles implicitly purveyed in the mass media, for example, but that those of us who listen to them are able to understand them, take them for our own and for the rest of the week often with no sense of inconsistency flout them at every turn. What Mill said is surely still true: that 'not one Christian in a thousand guides or tests his individual conduct' by 'the maxims and precepts contained in the New Testament'. His behaviour is rather informed, as Mill goes on to say, by 'the custom of his nation, his class, or his religious profession' (J. S. Mill, 'On Liberty', p. 168).

In proposing his second reason to account for intellectual secularisation, MacIntyre reminds us that even in medieval times, when there was no question of doubting Christianity, the internal incoherencies of Christian concepts were recognised and acutely discussed. Much thought was devoted, for example, to the apparent incompatibility between predestination and human freedom. Yet these incoherencies were regarded not as grounds for disbelief, but as no more than 'difficulties' and incentives to enquiry. MacIntyre's argument is that this was because the concepts in question 'were part of a set of concepts which were indispensable to the forms of description used in social and intellectual life'. But those forms of description have since become secularised, and so the incoherencies are now left 'high and dry' (MacIntyre, [2] p. 129).

He gives as an example of change affecting forms of description in this way the replacement of Aristotelian physics, which relied on the concept of a Prime Mover, by a physics which had no reliance of this kind. Such a development 'secularizes a whole area of enquiry', says MacIntyre. 'It weakens the hold of the concept of God on our intellectual life by showing that in this area we can dispense with descriptions which have any connection with the concept' (MacIntyre, [2] p. 129).

I think what I have said myself is not incompatible with this view. My argument has been that with the rise of science it became impossible to describe parts of the world or any of the things that happen in it in terms of 'the Supernatural' and that this process, draining 'the Supernatural' of empirical content, drained it at the same time of meaning. In MacIntyre's terms, we might say that replacing 'supernatural' descriptions of things by descriptions with no such reference 'weakens the hold of the concept of God (a "supernatural" being) on our intellectual life'.

It may be worth noting that MacIntyre's argument effectively emphasises a feature of our system of concepts which the

22

early verificationists were charged, rightly, I think, with neglecting: and that is the fact that they *do* form a 'system'. The criterion of verifiability as it was expressed in Ayer's 'Language, Truth and Logic' applied explicitly to *individua* purported propositions (see Ayer, p. 35). It was proposed to take individual sentences on their own, as independent entities, as it were, and apply the test of verifiability to each in turn. And the concept *God* was supposed to be exposed as bogus because the proposition which asserted God's existence could not be put to the test of experience (Ayer, p. 115).

Against this atomistic view of propositions and concepts, and against the sharp distinction between analytic and synthetic truths with which it is closely associated, W. V. O. Quine has suggested, for our conceptual framework, the analogy of a field of force (in 'Two Dogmas of Empiricism').

Concepts have to be considered as interconnected through a network of relationships, this view suggests, such that changes in one concept are likely to carry over to the neighbouring ones. But the degree of involvement varies. Some concepts are so central to our outlook that any change affecting them has repercussions throughout the whole conceptual structure (the notion of an 'individual' might be an example); while others can be changed with few and relatively trivial implications beyond themselves (the notion of a penny, for example).

The specific point of interest for us is that this view implies that it is quite possible for a concept (and thus a statement employing it) which is not open to direct empirical check nevertheless to be meaningful in virtue of its relations with other concepts which directly, or again indirectly, bear upon experience.

Hence our concern in the above with all things 'supernatural', and not just the one 'supernatural' being, God. We rely on the argument not that 'God' has no empirical content, but, to use Quine's metaphor, that all the areas over which what we might call 'the supernaturalist' world-view contacted experience have been done away with.

With quite remarkable percipience, the intelligent Mr Glanvill foresaw the developments we have sketched in the early days of scientific revolution. His spirited defence of the reality of witchcraft (in 'Sadducismus Triumphatus') came at a time when men of education were beginning to adopt an enlightened scientific scepticism towards it. Glanvill was by no means an obscurantist, and in general he embraced the new ways of thinking with an enthusiasm second to none. Yet married to his fervour for science was a fear for religion; for he saw then that science threatened one day to eliminate the category of 'the Supernatural' altogether, and what he sought to prevent was the first step in that process. 'Atheism is begun in *Sadducism*,' he wrote, 'and those that dare not bluntly say, There is No GOD, content themselves (for a fair step and Introduction) to deny that there are Spirits and Witches' (quoted by Basil Willey in 'The Seventeenth Century Background', p. 195). In my view, he could hardly have been more perceptive.

STOP

2 Religion without 'The Beyond'

> 'I don't believe that any religion can survive which is not a religion of the supernatural. . . .'
>
> T. S. Eliot

We no longer have a coherent concept of the supernatural: that is the gist of our argument so far. But Christianity is (or was) a 'supernatural' religion. Must we say therefore that Christianity is doomed? Several attempts have been made to explain how the answer 'No' can be returned to this question, even if the thesis of our first section is accepted; and to a consideration of the more important of them we now turn.

1 R. B. Braithwaite

If you accept that the concept of the supernatural is no longer coherent, more than one attitude to seeming propositions which purport to state facts about 'the Supernatural' ('God created heaven and earth', for example) are open to you. One possibility is to dismiss them as not propositions at all, but meaningless concatenations of words. This is the position of the Ayer of 'Language, Truth and Logic' and the logical positivists. A second possibility is to regard them as not about things 'supernatural' as they appear to be, but about things of *this* world. Later we shall discuss some writings of John Wisdom which, I hope it is fair to say, represent this alternative. Thirdly, the seeming-propositions of theologians may be interpreted as not stating (alleged) facts but rather as doing something else – prescribing, announcing intentions or telling stories, for example.

This third possibility is the one explored in Professor Braithwaite's famous lecture 'An Empiricist's View of Religious Belief' (first published in 1955). Religious assertions are to be understood, on Braithwaite's view, as being 'primarily declarations of adherence to a policy of action, declarations of commitment to a way of life' (Braithwaite, p. 239). An individual religious assertion does not, of course, itself specify a

25

programme of action, but the body of assertions which each individual assertion belongs to *does*, thinks Braithwaite, specify a particular way of life, and it is to this that a speaker commits himself on making a religious assertion.

But on Braithwaite's view religious assertions have a 'propositional element' too. They refer to what he calls *stories*, which he defines as propositions or sets of propositions which are 'capable of empirical test and which are thought of by the religious man in connection with his resolution to follow the way of life advocated by his religion' (Braithwaite, p. 244).

Braithwaite illustrates what he means when he talks of 'stories' by quoting Matthew Arnold's 'empirical interpretation' of the Christian doctrine of Justification by Atonement: God is interpreted as 'a sort of infinitely magnified and improved Lord Shaftesbury' and his son as a younger Lord Shaftesbury who sacrifices the joy of living with his Father to earn the salvation of those who would otherwise suffer the disastrous consequences of his Father's justice. This puts the atonement doctrine 'verificationally', says Braithwaite, in terms of human beings who may never have existed yet who nevertheless 'would have been empirically observable had they existed' (Braithwaite, p. 246). Christians differ in the empirical interpretations they give to doctrines, but this is alleged to be of no consequence since it is not necessary for any of the interpretations to be *believed*. The Christian is characterised by his '*entertainment*' of such stories, not by his regarding any of them as true.

Braithwaite summarises his position in this way: 'a religious assertion, for me, is the assertion of an intention to carry out a certain behaviour policy . . . together with the implicit or explicit statement, but not the assertion, of certain stories' (Braithwaite, p. 250).

Here then we have one attempt to answer the verificationist challenge we explored in the first section: an attempt which recognising the difficulty of treating the typical affirmations of the Christian religion as straightforwardly factual argues that their significance is nonetheless important.

A basic philosophical weakness is, I think, that it suspends itself from a 'use' theory of meaning which will not bear the strain. Surprisingly in view of its popularity, attempts to give such a theory precise formulation are exceedingly scarce.

Wittgenstein himself merely sketched an approach (in 'Philosophical Investigations'); W. P. Alston's account (now available as chapter 2 of his 'Philosophy of Language') is systematic and interesting, but pioneering (as he himself points out) rather than conclusive; while (we must admit) very recently there has appeared John Searle's valuable discussion in 'Speech Acts' (§ 6.4, inter alia). But the confidence with which Braithwaite wrote of 'the use principle', particularly in view of the *time* of writing, was hardly warranted. What little independent support Braithwaite himself provides for the 'theory' is of doubtful worth. He says that '. . . moral statements have a use in guiding conduct; and if they have a use they surely have a meaning – in some sense of meaning' (Braithwaite, p. 235). But surely there are many things that have uses but not meanings – my hat, for example.

There is of course a limit to the lengths one can take a theory of religious belief within the bounds of a single lecture: and yet one feels that E. L. Mascall has a legitimate objection when he complains in his book 'Words and Images' that Braithwaite fails to distinguish the different sorts of 'stories' that there seem to be in Christianity, and that while his theory is plausible in connection with some it is much less so in connection with others.

To begin with there are the Gospel parables, according well with what Braithwaite has to say, since not even the orthodox would want to argue that their point relied on their being true. But there are also stories 'deliberately constructed by a theologian in order to bring out some aspect of God's being or of his dealings with men; such, for example, is . . . the story of the Atonement as the paying of a fine in a criminal court on behalf of a bankrupt convict' (Mascall, [2] p. 56). It is not clear, thinks Mascall, how Braithwaite would regard these. But a third kind of 'story' – including apparently commonplace assertions about Jesus' life, such as that he was born in Bethlehem – Braithwaite would presumably, thinks Mascall, have to treat in the way that he treats the 'stories' with which he *does* explicitly deal: he would have to hold that 'it is very important to think about them, but quite irrelevant whether any of them is true' (Mascall, [2] p. 57). Thus Mascall reduces Braithwaite's doctrine to what he clearly regards as the absurd.

Mascall points out further that there would seem to be nothing in the way of a Braithwaitian Christian being a

Braithwaitian Buddhist and perhaps a Braithwaitian Hindu at the same time, so long as the associated moralities are compatible: for where it is 'stories' rather than people which are being entertained there is no obvious limit to the number which one person can cater for.

We may add, moreover, that since each believer in Braithwaite's view (Braithwaite, p. 245) is free to interpret the Christian stories as he thinks fit (so long as his interpretation is in terms of empirical propositions) the distinction between what orthodoxy regards as different religions is in danger of obliteration. For if the individual is quite free to arrive at his own interpretation how can there be preserved criteria for distinguishing between an interpretation of a Christian doctrine and an interpretation of, say, a Buddhist one? Indeed, the very notion of an 'interpretation' is put in jeopardy.

In connection with Mascall's criticism it may be worth noticing that a preliminary remark of his seems to reveal a strange misunderstanding of Braithwaite's position. He says that 'there seems to be no reason why the stories to which he refers should not only be entertained but should also be affirmed as true, since he himself says that all the propositions which they contain are empirical' (Mascall, [2] p. 55).

Yet the reason seems clear enough: Braithwaite (as a Christian) cannot affirm his 'stories' as true because he knows that many of them are false. Treating them as empirical is a device for securing their intelligibility, not their truth.

Mascall, however, is oddly explicit in attributing his invalid criticism to Mr T. H. McPherson: so perhaps his passing the remark is no more than an unusually subtle way of poking a friend.

Most commentators, however, have found Mascall's fundamental objection – that Braithwaite's position is seriously at odds with what is known as Christianity – reasonable enough. Christianity is clearly more than a set of moral principles, it has been urged, and the 'more' is certainly not the 'entertainment' of 'stories' which may or may not be true. To this question of how you tell a valid interpretation of Christianity from an invalid one we shall have to return (pp. 49 ff.); suffice it to say here that one has great sympathy with the view that Braithwaite's 'solution' is ingenious, bold and at the same time plainly bizarre.

The book Dr John Robinson thought well of – Paul van Buren's 'The Secular Meaning of the Gospel' – attempts to work out in some detail a slightly different theological position compatible with the conceptual developments we outlined in our first chapter. Van Buren accepts that 'the idea of the empirical intervention of a supernatural "God" in the world of men has been ruled out by the influence of modern science in our thinking' (van Buren, p. 100), but instead of hearing this as the death knell of theology, he hears it as calling only for a 'reinterpretation'. Christianity must be pruned of all its 'metaphysical', 'supernatural', 'other-worldly', non-empirical' or, as he sometimes puts it, 'cosmological' branches, but we shall in the end be left with a stock representing the 'essential meaning' of the Gospels and the Church's understanding of them, a stock which will possess the necessary vigour to survive and flourish in our secular world.

Paul van Buren's resulting formulation is very like Braith-waite's, as he himself is happy to point out. Statements of faith, he says, are to be interpreted '. . . as statements which express, describe, or commend a particular way of seeing the world, other men, and oneself, and the way of life appropriate to such a perspective' (van Buren, p. 156). And of course 'the world' referred to here is *this* world: 'statements of faith' cannot be understood today as referring to anything that has the least hint of 'the Supernatural' about it. He believes that the 'particular way of seeing the world' which a Christian enjoys is given by the biography of Jesus. In his own words: 'the norm of the Christian perspective is the series of events to which the New Testament documents testify, centering in the life, death and resurrection of Jesus of Nazareth' (van Buren, p. 156). The Christian acquires this perspective in a moment of 'discernment' (a term van Buren borrows from Ian Ramsey – see his 'Religious Language'), in which the life of Jesus is suddenly seen in a new light, revealing it as holding 'the key to the meaning of history'. At the same time the new Christian 'catches' the 'freedom' which was the distinctive mark of Jesus' character; that is to say, he reorients his life so as to follow the path of 'freedom' shown by Jesus himself.

In reading the details of van Buren's argument at least one

reader often gains the impression of ingenious sophistry. This is the kind of charge which space allows only to be illustrated, and I shall have to limit myself to two examples.

One problem which arises for any theology and in particular for van Buren's is this: 'Does the Gospel speak of a "saving" event which has happened already and which is reported to the listener, who is invited to acknowledge and give thanks for it . . . or does it announce the possibility of a "saving" event which takes place in the act of acknowledging it . . . ?' (van Buren, p. 152). Van Buren wants to argue that this is in fact a false antithesis, and that both 'alternatives' are true.

It is clear, I think, from our exposition that in van Buren's view the individual Christian is liberated when he 'catches the freedom of Jesus' and sees the world in a new perspective in a 'moment of discernment'. And from this it seems plain that he will have to deny that salvation or liberation happened once and for all in the life, death and resurrection of Jesus, plumping instead for the second alternative of those we indicated.

Yet it turns out that he wants to keep his cake as well as eating it – he wants to assert the first alternative as well as the second. He argues thus: 'It belongs to the language of a discernment situation as containing already ("objectively"), prior to its becoming the occasion of discernment, what was only "seen" at a later time' (van Buren, p. 153). He then cites as an analogous case that of a lover seeing his beloved's beauty for the first time. Though prepared to admit that he hadn't noticed it before the 'discernment situation' which comprised his falling in love, he would nevertheless insist, says van Buren, that she had *been* beautiful all along.

But, in the Christian's case, what is it that he sees in his moment of discernment? Van Buren has told us that what he sees is Jesus' life and death as 'the key to history'; and just as the lover would say his beloved had been beautiful all along, so the new convert might well say that Jesus' biography had comprised the 'key to history' all along, although he had only just *seen* it.

But this says nothing about the convert's *liberation*. It is not his *liberation* that he sees in the discernment situation; liberation is something according to van Buren that the convert *catches*, not something that he *sees*. And so there would be no temptation whatever on the part of the newly converted Christian to say

30

that his liberation 'had been there all along'. Van Buren's argument thus hangs on a confusion between two things he has carefully distinguished elsewhere – seeing the world in a new light and 'catching Jesus' freedom', a confusion aided and abetted by a misleading analogy.

For a second example consider what van Buren says about the disciples', and in particular Peter's, claim to have seen Jesus at the first Easter. 'He appeared to me', and 'I saw him', van Buren tells us, 'both record sensations of appearance. We may call them both "sense-content" statements. . . .' But '. . . the way to verify a statement of sense-content is to see if the words and actions of the person who makes the statement conform to it', so that 'Peter's statement of sense-content, which identified the one he saw with a man who had lived a certain kind of life, is verified by Peter's subsequent life'. Van Buren wants thus to assert that Jesus' not being there does not count against someone's claim to have seen him. In the terms of another example, van Buren says explicitly that my claim to have seen John in the station yesterday is not invalidated 'simply by the fact that John wasn't there. . . . I would have no grounds for saying I did not see what I saw' (van Buren, pp. 129, 130).

But isn't this obviously wrong? Van Buren obliterates a perfectly familiar, highly useful distinction between 'I saw N' and 'I thought I saw N' for no better reason than the preservation of his theological extravaganza. *Of course* John's not being in the station counts against my claim to have seen him: if he wasn't there *I can't* have seen him. And if Jesus wasn't there on Easter morning then *he* couldn't have been seen either (although, equally obviously, people may have *thought* they saw him).

To a man professedly so concerned with 'linguistic analysis' it may also be worth pointing out that all the great play made with Jesus' 'freedom' amounts to little more than a linguistic conjuring trick. Whenever a man does one thing when he might have done another we can say he was *free* to do it; whenever a man lacks a quality we can say he is free of it; and whenever particular constraints do not restrict a man we can say he is *free* of them. Clearly therefore we are all 'free' in an unlimited number of ways; and in fact the word is such that until we have said *in what respects* a man is free, to apply the adjective alone is

31

virtually meaningless. And yet where van Buren does mention respects, it is with an air of illustration rather than specification (van Buren, pp. 121–3).

Two issues which arise in van Buren's case as in Braithwaite's are his reliance on a 'use' theory of meaning and his claim to be giving an interpretation of *Christianity*. We shall come back to the latter in part later; but meanwhile, if further exploration of the weakness of van Buren's position is wanted we are fortunate in being able to refer to E. L. Mascall's excellent discussion in 'The Secularization of Christianity' (ch. ii). It is remarkable, I think, that Mascall keeps a clear head throughout his dissection of van Buren's views, since it is plain from his general position and from the occasional wry remark that he finds them extremely unsympathetic. But his treatment is careful, and even fair, from beginning to end, with the result that he has produced a critique of the details of van Buren's position which it would be difficult to better.

3 The Death of Godders

As we leave van Buren we may pause to explain our neglect of those whom some regard as his colleagues in the American Death of God movement. The principal of these we take to be Gabriel Vahanian, Harvey Cox, Thomas Altizer and William Hamilton. They cannot figure centrally in these pages since for all their ultra-radical image none of them seems to take seriously the view that the idea of a 'supernatural' God has become meaningless.

In Vahanian and Cox this is obvious. They both explicitly believe in 'God', though they feel that our modern situation calls for an unusual expression of that belief. Cox's strength (such as it is) in any case lies in his sociology; when he turns to specifically theological questions, as in the last chapter of 'The Secular City', his remarks, I think, are less than helpful.

Altizer on the other hand is adamant that we are to recognise 'the death of God as a historical event. . . . God is not simply hidden from view, nor is he lurking in the depths of our unconscious or on the boundaries of our infinite space, nor will he appear on the next turn of a historical wheel of fate. . . . The contemporary Christian must accept the death of God as a final and irrevocable event' (Altizer and Hamilton, 'Radical Theology and the Death of God', p. 129). This is clear enough; but a good deal of what Altizer goes on to say is less so. Having stressed in this passage the finality and irreversibility of the death of God, he yet feels free to assert elsewhere that 'the death of God . . . must lead to a repetition of the Resurrection, to a new epiphany of the New Being' (quoted in B. Murchland (ed.), 'The Meaning of the Death of God', p. 33). Moreover, he allows himself to speak of 'The God beyond the Christian God, beyond the God of the historic Church, beyond all which Christendom has known as God' (Murchland, p. 34). These remarks, and those of which they are representative, have led at least two critics to question the thoroughness with which Altizer has in the end accepted the meaninglessness of 'God'. J. W. Montgomery writes, for example, that 'though Altizer outbarths Barth in his employment of the transcendence principle, thus apparently leaving the "soft" radicals [Vahanian and Cox] far behind, his affirmation of God's death is, after all, still a dialectic affirmation: from the ashes of God's pyre will rise, like the Phoenix, a "God beyond God" ' (J. W. Montgomery, 'A Philosophical-Theological Critique of the Death of God Movement', p. 35). And Hamilton argues that Altizer's vision, 'beginning with man accepting, affirming, even willing the death of God in a radical sense, ends with man willing to participate in the utter desolation of the secular or the profane, willing to undergo the discipline of darkness, the dark night of the soul . . . while *the possibility of a new epiphany of the sacred, a rebirth of the possibility of having God once more is awaited*' (Altizer and Hamilton, p. 43; my italics).

Hamilton himself, though, manifests the very same vacillation: in some places he writes like a thoroughgoing radical, accepting the unintelligibility of the concept of the 'supernatural' or the 'transcendent'; in others, he seems happy to go on using terms which depend on them. On page 53 of the Altizer and Hamilton volume we find him declaring that 'the death of God must be affirmed'; and again on page 49: 'My Protestant [i.e. the man with whom Hamilton agrees] has no God, has no faith in God, and affirms both the death of God and the death of all forms of theism.' And yet having thus started bravely on the secular path, Hamilton suddenly loses all his nerve, performs an abrupt about-turn and skips back to the theistic fold: 'there is an element of expectation, even hope, that removes my position from classical atheisms', he explains. 'If God is not needed, if it is to the world and not God that we repair for our needs and problems, then perhaps *we may come to see that he is to be enjoyed and delighted in.* Part of the meaning of waiting for God is found in this attempt to understand what delighting in him might mean ... our waiting for God, our godlessness, is partly a search for a language and style by which we might be enabled to stand before him once again, delighting in his presence' (Altizer and Hamilton, p. 53; my italics). Too clearly we see that what distinguishes Hamilton's position 'from classical atheisms' is its theism.

Altizer especially and Hamilton also draw on a theologico-philosophical tradition which is different from the one behind the present essay, and this makes brief exposition and comment in this context impossible. Any real discussion would very quickly have to descend to the level of basic presuppositions. All we have tried to do, by quotation, is to hint that these writers may not be as radical as sometimes they sound, and that consequently they may not in fact be discussing the loss of 'the Supernatural' as we understand it.

4 John Wisdom

Those who regard the notion of the supernatural as strictly incoherent may take the view, as we suggested at the beginning of this section, that when people seem to talk about the 'supernatural' world they are in reality talking in a covert way about the *secular* world. But for those who attempt this approach the following problem arises: from what religious believers can be heard saying, it seems that they regard their beliefs as independent of any fact that can be experimentally established. (For example, the fact that there is much suffering in the world does not prevent them believing 'that God loves his creatures'.) Yet if this is the case, how is it possible for religious beliefs to be construed as factual assertions about this world?

John Wisdom answers by saying that there can be facts in the world which are not establishable by experiment (construed widely); and it is among this non-experimental kind of fact that the facts religion alleges are to be found.

34

Logic and mathematics, he says, provide examples of 'non-experimental' facts: checking is done by reworking the calculation or derivation, not by reconducting any experiments. But more interesting examples, from the present point of view, are to be found in the law courts and in aesthetic debates.

Wisdom seems unsure or unfussy whether to call the truths he wants to draw attention to in these cases 'facts' or not: his interest is to show that they are propositions which can properly be assessed as *right* or *wrong* ('Gods', p. 156; also 'Religious Belief', p. 54) and which can be supported or attacked by recognised procedures ('Gods', p. 159). In an effort to be clear on this point I shall in what follows introduce a bracketed 'experimental' where the facts being referred to seem to be of the kind that may be settled by further observation or experiment, in contrast to the kind which remain unsettled even when all relevant empirical evidence is available.

In 'Gods' Wisdom takes his court case example first. 'In courts of law,' he says, 'it sometimes happens that opposing counsel are agreed as to the [experimental] facts and are not trying to settle a question of further [experimental] fact. They may be concerned with 'whether Mr. A who admittedly handed his long-trusted clerk signed blank cheques did or did not exercise reasonable care, whether a ledger is or is not a document, whether a certain body was or was not a public authority' ('Gods', p. 157).

I may add that there is an excellent example of this kind of case in Jacob Epstein's 'Autobiography', where for customs purposes it became important whether a certain metallic article was to be classed as a work of art, or as 'a manufacture in metal'. The article in question was the work of Constantin Brancusi, which he had called 'The Bird', and it stood in full view of the court which sat to decide the question. In a sense, 'the facts' were indisputable; yet in another sense the question of whether 'in fact' the thing was a work of art or not was what occupied the lawyers for something over two years (Epstein, pp. 131–5).

The important thing to notice about these cases is that they result not in the establishment of a hitherto unestablished (experimental) fact to which the various evidences could be regarded as clues (as in a whodunnit), but rather in the attaching of a label, a decision as to which category the act or object in question properly comes under, a ruling as to which

35

concept shall properly be applied. 'The logic of [this kind of] dispute', says Wisdom, is not 'a matter of collecting from several inconclusive items of information an expectation as to something further, as when a doctor from a patient's symptoms guesses at what is wrong, or a detective from many clues guesses the criminal. It has its own sort of logic and its own sort of end – the solution of the question at issue is a decision, a ruling by the judge' ('Gods', pp. 157–8).

Yet, Wisdom goes on, this is true only in a sense. For the attempt to settle the dispute will consist in the parties agreeing to look again, to trace out for each other the patterns they see, to explain to each other the features they take to be especially important, and so on. In the Brancusi case, for example, some of the witnesses stressed the irrelevance of the agreed fact that in spite of its name, the sculpture looked very little like a 'bird', and indeed very little like anything else, while others, called by the other side, urged that all *bona fide* sculpture was representational and that in particular 'The Bird' should live up to its name. Here, what will settle the issue is one party 'coming to see' the irrelevance of a matter he had hitherto taken to be important (or vice versa).

Furthermore, Wisdom points out, claims that seem to be about the existence of a god or gods, about the existence of 'divine minds', must surely be closely related to claims about the existence of human (and animal) minds; and so there is a third kind of statement which bears illuminating resemblances to what are alleged to be religious statements. Just as the assertion that there are other minds besides my own is supported by there being a distinctive kind of pattern in human and animal behaviour, so the proposition that there are gods depends on whether there are 'other mind-patterns in nature beside the human and animal patterns which we can all easily detect' and on whether 'these other mind-patterns are superhuman' ('Gods', pp. 151–2).

Where should we look for these patterns which will enable us to speak truly of gods? Wisdom says: among human reactions. There are, he tells us, 'patterns in human reactions which are well described by saying that we are as if there were hidden within us powers, persons, not ourselves and stronger than ourselves' ('Gods', p. 166). (Elsewhere, one might point out, he says that patterns in the world at large are also relevant to the

36

question of the existence of gods (e.g. 'The Logic of God', pp. 12, 13).)

As a preliminary remark we may notice that while it would be unjust to charge Wisdom with attempting to explain one obscurity by invoking another, his *explicans*, to say the least of it, has difficulties all of its own. His account of how religious assertions are to be understood, that is to say, relies partly on paralleling them with assertions about *minds*. Just as we speak of minds in virtue of distinctive patterns in human behaviour, so, Wisdom suggests, we may speak of gods in virtue of other patterns displayed by human behaviour and in the world at large. But the problem of understanding what is meant by speaking of minds has itself occupied philosophers for centuries – and Wisdom himself for a good while, if we are to judge from his writings on the subject (see 'Other Minds') – so that using talk about minds to explain how we are to take talk about gods can only be less than fully illuminating.

5 Phillips' critique

Recently, Wisdom's view has come under more sustained attack from what may be called the Neo-Wittgensteinian position, represented in this case by D. Z. Phillips though on other occasions by Peter Winch, Norman Malcolm, Roy Holland and J. R. Jones. The school of thought (as concerns religious matters) reflected in the writings of these authors is in a comparatively undeveloped state. It emerges as a distinctive view partly from hints thrown out in writings devoted in the main to other topics (I am thinking here principally of Winch's writings, 'The Idea of a Social Science' and 'Understanding a Primitive Society'), but even where it receives explicit and sustained treatment (chiefly one supposes in Phillips' 'The Concept of Prayer') what it is anxious to deny is communicated much more clearly than what it is prepared to assert.

The Neo-Wittgensteinian agrees with the first two writers we considered – Braithwaite and van Buren – in recognising that statements about God cannot be taken as straightforwardly factual ones. The logical positivists argued that factual statements had to be open to empirical verification, and drew the conclusion that theological statements were not factual and therefore (since not analytic either) meaningless. Braithwaite and van Buren accepted that the criterion of empirical verifiability picked out factual statements, and that this meant that theological statements were not factual; but in their view statements (if 'statement' is the right word) could be meaningful even though neither factual nor analytic. They then proceeded to explain the distinctive sort of meaning they thought such 'statements' had.

Phillips, whom we might take as a representative Neo-Wittgensteinian, agrees with this (though doubtless for different reasons), except that the distinctive kind of meaning he sees religious statements as having is different from that attributed to them by either Braithwaite or van Buren.

What kind of a meaning then does Phillips see religious statements as having? It would, I think, be entirely against the spirit of his approach to expect to this question an answer which could be neatly and shortly formulated. Instead, we are offered first the advice: '. . . look to see what men do with things, with words and with ideas, and observe their behaviour' (Phillips quotes this from W. Watson's 'On Understanding Physics' (see 'The Concept of Prayer' ,p. 7)) and second, in Phillips' case, the example provided by the rest of the book. Perhaps what is distinctive about the Neo-Wittgensteinian position, as well as what is distinctive about Wisdom's view, will emerge if we now consider Phillips' exemplary critique of the latter, which he calls 'Wisdom's Gods'.

Phillips' basic disagreement with Wisdom, I think, centres on whether religious beliefs can be regarded as beliefs about 'what is the case'. The 'scare' quotation marks around this phrase are of course well deserved: a large part of the difficulty in choosing between Wisdom and Phillips lies in getting clear about it.

One of the ways Phillips has of putting their disagreement is to urge that in Wisdom's account religious beliefs are treated as 'hypotheses'. 'Because Wisdom holds that the reality expressed by beliefs about God is to be found in certain patterns of human reactions, those beliefs are for him, at best, hypotheses.' But, Phillips goes on, 'do Christians speak of their beliefs about God as hypotheses which may or may not be true? It seems pretty clear that they do not. Their beliefs are absolutes for them' ('Wisdom's Gods', p. 27).

I think Phillips' use of the term 'hypotheses' in this connection is unfortunate, since it can mislead a superficial reader (myself in this case – I have to thank Dr R. S. Woolhouse for making this clear) into thinking that the argument is as follows: for Wisdom, religious beliefs hang on what is the case; they are therefore hypotheses; hypotheses are necessarily tentative; but Christians clearly do not regard their beliefs as tentative (they are 'absolutes for them'): therefore, something is wrong with Wisdom's account.

It would then hang on the extraordinary doctrine that all contingent truths – truths 'dependent on what happens to be the case' – are 'hypotheses', only to be believed tentatively by the sensible person. And this would obviously be untenable. That I live in Wales is a contingent truth: but I do not entertain it tentatively. In any normal sense, surely, it is not a hypothesis.

Perhaps a better understanding of Phillips' meaning emerges from what he goes on to say about forgiveness. We are invited to consider the saying of Jesus that 'if ye forgive men their trespasses your heavenly Father will also forgive you' (Matthew 6: 14). The sense in which this should properly be taken, says Phillips, is given by Kierkegaard when he asserts that 'your forgiveness of another is your own forgiveness' (Kierkegaard, quoted in Phillips, [2] p. 28). God's forgiving a man is not something that happens after and as a separate happening from the man's forgiving: both happen at once – or, rather, there is only *one* happening which is both a man's forgiving the trespasses of those who trespass against him and God's forgiving *him*: 'if honestly before God you wholeheartedly forgive your enemy . . . then you dare hope also for your forgiveness, for it is one and the same' (Kierkegaard, quoted in Phillips, [2] p. 28).

Phillips is arguing that religious truths, of which Jesus' saying about forgiveness is an example, are not of the kind Wisdom takes them for. They are not to do with 'what in fact is the case'; their truth is not, as Wisdom implies that it is, 'a matter of factual enquiry'.

It may be no more than a superficial linguistic objection to suggest that surely Kierkegaard is trying to tell us something 'that is the case' about forgiveness, and that if what he says is true, surely it would be perfectly natural to say that it constituted 'a fact' about forgiveness. The notions of *what is the case*, a *truth*, and a *fact* are used in ordinary language to do too many jobs for them to be employed by Phillips to reflect the distinction he has in mind.

Yet in a sense it is clear that there is a distinction between the kind of truth Kierkegaard seems to be trying to express and the kind of truth we would be expressing if we said, for example: if you let all your debtors off, the chances are that when you are called on to pay up, your creditor will take a lenient view.

But what *is* this distinction? What kind of truth *is* it that Kierkegaard is attempting to express? It cannot be a truth about human psychology, for then it would presumably be 'a matter of factual enquiry'. It is surely not a conceptual truth, analogous to our saying that there can only be forgiveness where someone has been wronged. Is it then a *moral* truth? Or an *aesthetic* one? No, I think Phillips is saying: the truth Kierkegaard is trying to express is a *religious* one. But the trouble lies in knowing what this means.

One thing that is distinctive about religious beliefs, on Phillips' view, comes out in his discussion of whether reasonable men can be expected, after exhaustive discussion, to reach agreement on them. Wisdom, he says, seems to think so: 'Does Wisdom think that . . . with sufficient patience eventual agreement will be forthcoming? . . . Wisdom's stress on the facts, on what is so, suggests that he would answer [this question] in the affirmative' (Phillips, [2] pp. 31–2).

For Phillips, then, it seems that where two rational people fail to agree on a question of religious belief it need not be that one is right and the other wrong – not because they can both be right at once, but because the notion of 'right or wrong' does not apply where the belief is a *religious* belief. Religious belief cannot be assessed in this dimension.

Religious belief and 'factual' belief are thus, in Phillips' view, of different kinds. In particular, religious belief is not a variety of 'factual' belief. It is *sui generis*. If, therefore, one wished to ask about the validity or appropriateness of a particular religious belief the criteria invoked would have to be religious ones. They could not be the same as those employed where it was particular 'factual' beliefs that were in question. Moreover, it would simply be incoherent to ask about the validity or appropriateness of religious beliefs *in general*: one could only do so by invoking criteria external to religion, which (if it is right to think that religious beliefs are *sui generis*) would be illegitimate. And so

40

Wisdom's whole project of enquiring into 'the reasonableness, the propriety of belief in gods' (Wisdom, [1] p. 163) comes under criticism: 'Wisdom', says Phillips, 'is seeking justifications beyond the point where it makes sense to do so' (Phillips, [2] p. 31).

6 *The autonomy of religion*

Undergirding Phillips' thesis about the autonomy of religious language and belief is a view that has its most explicit development in the writings of another Neo-Wittgensteinian, Peter Winch. It is the view that criteria of intelligibility, rationality and reality are to be found within what Winch, following Wittgenstein, calls each 'form of life'.

Winch puts this claim forward in connection with his account of what is involved in 'understanding' a society; and the particular example he takes is that of the African people, the Azande. What he wants to insist on is that it is illegitimate to appraise the Azande way of life by invoking concepts of *rationality* and *reality* which have developed within *our* culture. We cannot properly say, for example, on the grounds that science has disproved it, that the Azande belief in Witchcraft is a mistaken belief. To do so would be to apply the criteria which (among others) we use to distinguish truth from falsity in *our* culture, to beliefs entertained in a different culture, a culture which has its own criteria for making this (or, we had better say, a 'parallel') distinction.

The argument that supports this thesis is that concepts gain their meaning by being embedded in forms of social life. Our concept of reality is what it is in virtue of the use to which it is put by people sharing a way of life together. Consequently, it only has meaning *within* that form of life; and it makes no sense either to apply it to activities and beliefs which belong to *another* form of life or to forms of life as a whole.

The relevance of this interesting argument to the understanding of religious 'statements' derives from the fact that some people have wanted the concept 'form of life' to apply not only to cultures *as a whole*, as it does in Winch's discussion of the Azande, but to activities going on *within* cultures: to religious activities in our society, for example.

41

Winch himself is one of these people. Science and religion are examples he gives of 'modes of social life' each of which 'has criteria of intelligibility peculiar to itself' ('The Idea of a Social Science', p. 100) and it is implied that there is just the same illegitimacy in trying to apply concepts of one mode of life to activities within another as there is in trying to apply concepts which have developed within one culture to features of other cultures. The beliefs and concepts of religion, to use the example of a 'mode of life' we are interested in, cannot be appraised from *outside* religion, but only from within: and this, I hope I am right in thinking, is the foundation stone of the Neo-Wittgensteinian's view.

Crucially involved in the argument thus developed is, as I have indicated, a transition from talk of a 'form of life' by which is meant something that is characteristic of an entire culture, to talk of a 'mode of social life' meaning an activity or set of activities going on *within* a culture: the transition from talk of the Azande way of life to talk of 'science' or 'religion' which are pursued *within* a way of life. This transition is scarcely justified in the writings we are referring to, not least, one is tempted to think, for the reason that it is not justifiable.

For it confuses at least two very different things. I shall use the two terms 'mode of social life' and 'form of life' to mark this distinction in what follows, in spite of the fact that they are used synonymously by Nielsen (in 'Wittgensteinian Fideism'), who is fairly reflecting what is, I think, implicit in Winch.

A 'form of life' I shall thus use to refer to the life-style of a culture – of which the social structure and functioning of Winch's (or, better, Evans-Pritchard's) Azande would be one example; and another, the form which civilisation takes in contemporary western Europe. To describe a 'form of life' would thus be to describe a culture: its class structure (if it had one), how power was distributed, the way in which the satisfaction of basic needs was institutionalised, the methods employed in maintaining order, the art which flourished, and so on. It might be possible for a given individual to 'move' from one form of life, in this sense, to another, but typically a given individual would engage in one form only – and in any event no one could change his 'form of life' at all frequently.

On the other hand, in the sense in which I shall use the term 'mode of social life', a single person might be involved in several

42

modes of social life in a single day. For by this phrase I shall refer to distinctive sorts of activities which go on *within* a single culture – *within* a single 'form of life'. A man might, for example, go to his office, lunch with his colleagues, attend Evensong in the Cathedral and call in at a political meeting at night.

It is relevant to notice that in each of these activities there would be to some extent a distinctive vocabulary, a distinctive set (open-ended) of actions which were appropriate, a distinctive set which were inappropriate, and, in a certain sense of 'logic', each would have to some extent a distinctive logic. 'Susan, there's an error in this typing!' which might be said in the office would have a different 'logic' from that of the lunchtime remark, 'Waiter, there's a fly in my soup!'

It has been suggested that the distinctive vocabulary and 'logic' we have spoken of as characterising different modes of social life form areas of discourse sufficiently distinguished from one another to be regarded as to some extent independent and self-sufficient palatinates within the nation that is the language of the culture. 'Realm of discourse' is the old-fashioned term employed in this connection, and though I daren't say that this is what is meant by Wittgenstein's notion of a language game, I will say that it represents an idea of the same sort. Nielsen uses the phrase 'mode of discourse', though not too helpfully he simply regards it as synonymous with 'form of life' – and indeed, with 'mode of social life' (Nielsen, pp. 200–1). In what follows I shall take it that a mode of discourse is the distinctive vocabulary and 'logic' which is associated with a mode of social life.

With these distinctions in mind, consider now the essential transition which the Wittgensteinian Fideist makes from claiming that criteria of intelligibility, reality and so on are necessarily internal to a way of life, to claiming that such criteria are also internal to modes of social life.

The argument for the first claim is that concepts have meaning in virtue of being embedded in a particular form of life. And this, I suggest, is plausible (I do not say I believe it) for the following reason: it is possible, simply by engaging in the form of life of a group of people to gain, in the end, a full understanding of their language (as children do, of course).

But the same argument does not apply to modes of social life and their associated modes of discourse. We could not learn the meaning of all the words which figured in a mode of discourse

43

simply by participating in the associated mode of social life.

One reason for this is that modes of discourse always rely to some extent on words which are not peculiar to them, but which occur in connection with other modes of social life too. In the case of the alleged religious mode of discourse we may borrow the examples MacIntyre takes in 'Is Understanding Religion Compatible with Believing?' (p. 116). These are the words 'wise' and 'powerful'. If it is right at all to think that words get their meaning from the role they play in social life it seems clear that these words in particular get at least part of their meaning from their use in contexts which have nothing to do with religion.

The present argument is, then, that because many words are, on their own, not in any sense distinctive of the mode of discourse in which they occur a person seeking a full understanding of them must engage in those other sorts of activities in connection with which they also occur.

But a second reason, which seems to apply with great force to the case we are primarily interested in – religion (should it be conceived of as a mode of social life at all) – is that even words which seem to be especially characteristic of this mode of discourse – e.g. 'salvation', 'love', 'grace', in Christianity's case – cannot be understood fully by someone engaging in this mode of social life *alone*. The Christian concept of 'love' for example is a concept which is supposed to have meaning in the whole of life.

You have to know something about politics before you can say what Christian love means in a political context; you have to know something of medicine and its practice to know what its implications are for the Christian doctor; and so on. But to understand these things you have to engage in the relevant activities. You cannot come to much of an understanding of Christian love, that is to say, without engaging in activities besides those associated with the 'mode of discourse' of Christianity.

The first of these two arguments shows that 'palatinate' is rather too strong a term to apply to 'modes of discourse': if there is justification for the notion at all, modes of discourse cannot be thought of in Nielsen's phrase as 'conceptually self-sufficient' (Nielsen, p. 201) – as independent of and isolated from the rest of the language. It can, after all, be badly misleading to speak of the 'language' of physics, the 'language' of politics or the 'language' of religion. There may well be features peculiar to the talk which goes on in each of these fields: but strictly speaking the language used in all of them will be the same.

My second argument however should perhaps best be construed as casting doubt on the legitimacy of regarding 'religion' as a mode of social life at all. For to regard it as such is to regard it as a *part* of life; and perhaps to regard religion as anything other than an orientation towards *everything* that one does is to be involved in 'deep misunderstanding'. Surely the Christian would maintain, with his lips at least, that while there *are* distinctively religious activities like going to Church and praying regularly and studying the Bible, their point lies partly outside themselves, in informing the entire way of life of the believer.

This shows, I think, that Christianity still hankers after the status of 'form of life' which it once enjoyed – in medieval times for example. With secularisation it has declined into a quasi-mode of social life. Still its believers pay lip service to its large claims of having a crucial bearing on *all* of life's activities, and yet can we doubt that for the vast majority of them it exerts not the *only* overriding claim but *one* claim among others? Can we doubt that for most modern Christians Christianity is a *part* of life, not an orientation towards the whole of it?

But I do not say this to criticise them. In chapter 1 I have given reasons for thinking that any 'supernaturalist' form of life is incompatible with a scientific culture, and it is a scientific culture to which for good or bad we belong. Any serious commitment to doing everything that one does religiously – to religion as a form of life, or as we say to 'the religious way of life' – leads straight, so it seems to me, to the monastery: that is, to a closed community as isolated as it can be from the secular conceptual framework as well as the secular ways of behaving which rule outside.

7 The Pelzs

Werner and Lotte Pelz will not, I think, thank me for bringing their intriguing book 'God is No More' into the present context of academic philosophising about religion. Theirs is a work more of poetry than of philosophy, and they betray the poet's disdain

45

for logic-chopping and the splitting of hairs – that is to say (I speak as a philosopher), for careful and rigorous thinking. Perhaps because of this, the Pelzs' book breaks upon the creased theological brow like a beaker full of clear spring-water. The words of Jesus, as the Pelzs share with us their vision of them, sparkle with a totally unexpected freshness.

The book urges that the 'God' of religion – of traditional Christianity – was not the God of Jesus. When Jesus spoke of 'God', 'Father' and 'Lord', it alleges, he was speaking parabolically: speaking about this world and this life. He was speaking of 'something to be grasped and understood only within the very movement of life. . . . If we seek to discover the reality of these sayings in any other way we shall be faced by a riddle without a solution, worse: by a word without meaning, the word 'God'. (No 'heavenly meaning' will make matters any clearer. It will rather obscure the living "earthly meaning".)' (W. and L. Pelz, p. 110). And when the disciples at the Last Supper quarrel about the seating arrangements in Jesus' kingdom, which they conceive of as a matter of the future, they show, say the Pelzs, their great misunderstanding: 'they do not realize that they have already got their kingdom, that it is already among them, sitting at their table, sharing a meal with them. The kingdom has come, they are in it, and they do not know it. They cannot acknowledge the free, spontaneous communion between man and man as their ultimate destiny' (W. and L. Pelz, p. 122).

This is one side of the Pelzs' message: that a man's perfect fulfilment is possible and only possible in his relationships with other people. Jesus' promise to his disciples was that 'in their mutual love they would find all they had ever hoped for' (W. and L. Pelz, p. 41).

But the 'hope' referred to here, man's 'eternal longings', seem to receive a very different understanding in other things that the Pelzs have to say. The difficulty that the Pelzs have to cope with is that if fulfilment of man's 'eternal longings' is to be found only in life, how are we to understand the apparently central tenet of Christianity that Jesus' death was somehow a *triumph*? Surely the Pelzs must regard it as the final dashing of any hopes he may have had?

In what I interpret as a denial of this implication, the Pelzs claim that in fact the life of Jesus 'has become – in spite of or

46

because of his death – a parable of hope' (W. and L. Pelz, p. 111). And this reminds us of what they say earlier on, that it was Jesus' teaching that 'this world is a parable, a symbol, a something that can only be described in a paradox . . . ' (W. and L. Pelz, p. 57).

In such words the Pelzs hint at something *beyond* life; they hint, despite what we have already heard them say, that man's eternal longings are not to be fully met in this life, but have their focus 'beyond' it. The nearest we get to an unambiguous statement (and it is of course not the least bit unambiguous) concerns the Resurrection, which represents, it is said, 'the challenge to take this life and this earth seriously, because everything is a parable, a beginning and not an end in itself' (W. and L. Pelz, p. 127).

I spoke earlier of the sparkle of the Pelzs' book: and I stress now that it is a sparkle which belongs to the poet and which it would be silly to attempt to evoke here. It will be clear from the brief remarks I have made that my difficulty lies not in criticising what these writers have to say, but in achieving a clear understanding of it; and I mention the book not because its highly idiosyncratic substance can be effectively summarised and discussed but because it represents a unique and stimulating reaction to the demise of a 'supernatural' 'God'.

8 Honest John Robinson

We have said nothing, and are about to say little, about the book which in England at any rate did so much to bring the issues we are here concerned with into live debate: John Robinson's 'Honest to God'. It is to be neglected not because it isn't (or perhaps better *wasn't*) in many ways a marvellous little book, but because the ways in which it is *not* marvellous are the ways in which we in this context must primarily be interested.

Its great value resided in the fact that it introduced to a large number of people a discussion of great importance as well as interest which had hitherto been confined to journals of academic theology; and this it did by being written in a popular and exciting style by a Bishop of the Established Church who seemed to be saying some highly unepiscopal things.

But when a chairman is attempting to stimulate a discussion he does not concern himself overmuch with consistency – he throws out ideas which he hopes will be suggestive and provoking: and so it is, I think, with 'Honest to God'. It is *not* a carefully worked out philosophical or theological work. It is *not* free of contradictions. It does *not* set forth a clear and unambiguous theological position.

E. L. Mascall makes a meal of these deficiencies, if deficiencies they be, in the sustained attack to be found in 'The Secularisation of Christianity'. From our point of view, the most relevant ambiguity he picks out is that between belief and disbelief in 'the transcendent'. In much of what he says, Robinson seems to insist that all 'supernatural' notions must be done away with as no longer intelligible, and that theological statements are to be construed as statements about this world. For example: 'To say that "God is personal" is to say that "reality at its very deepest level is personal". . . . theological statements are not a description of "the highest Being" but an analysis of the depths of personal relationships – or, rather, an analysis of the depths of *all* experience "interpreted by love". Theology, as Tillich insists, is about "that which concerns us ultimately" ' (Robinson, pp. 48–9).

Yet in other places, Robinson stresses that any theist must retain the concept of 'transcendence': 'the question of God is the question of transcendence' (Robinson, p. 51). In some places in explaining what he means by 'transcendence' Robinson sounds like an orthodox theologian; but more often he relies on metaphors which have their inverted commas removed but never explained away. 'Theological statements are indeed affirmations about human existence,' he says, ' – but they are affirmations about the ultimate ground and depth of that existence' (Robinson, p. 52). Elsewhere he declares, in orthodox style: '. . . we are united to the source, sustainer and goal of our life in a relationship whose only analogy is that of *I* to *Thou* – except that the freedom in which we are held is one of utter dependence. . . . It is this freedom', he goes on, more colourfully, 'which gives us (within the relationship of dependence) the independence, the "distance", as it were, to be ourselves' (Robinson, p. 131).

Mascall, as I have said, reveals the weaknesses and inadequacies of Robinson's argument with skill, with wit, and

48

without mercy. At the same time, though, he reveals his own utter lack of appreciation of the intellectual pressures – the chief of which I have tried to describe in the first chapter of this essay – which led Robinson to write as he did. (See, as one indication of this, the quotation from Mascall above p. 12.) They are pressures which very many of us have felt; and some of us at least are grateful to Robinson for his vigorous expression of worries half-formed at the back of our minds and for the stimulation his book gave to our thoughts.

9 'Interpreting' Christianity

The repeated, and to most of us readily intelligible, charge of conservatism against the New Theologians is the old-fashioned one of *heresy*. What they preach, it is said, may be sincerely believed; it may be relevant to modern concerns; it may be 'meaningful' to contemporary people; but it is not Christianity.

The acute question therefore arises: what criteria can be appealed to in claiming that a would-be 'interpretation' of Christianity is not in reality Christianity at all? How can we distinguish a *version* of Christianity from a doctrine or set of doctrines which is *similar* to Christianity without being identical with it?

Take one of the more bizarre interpretations that have recently been offered. In 'The Secular City' Harvey Cox writes that 'the formulation of the Council of Chalcedon held that Jesus was fully God *and* fully man. When the same discussion is translated into the vocabulary of contemporary social change, the issue is whether history, and particularly revolution, is something that happens *to* man or something that man *does*' (Cox, p. 111). Now I think this is a quite astonishing 'translation'. But the question is: How might my astonishment be justified? or: How might it be eased? How could it be shown that Cox was here retaining the substance of the Chalcedon doctrine while modernising its formulation?

We should distinguish, I think, between two enterprises that may prima facie be afoot when someone begins an attempt at 'interpretation'. Consider the case we have already had occasion to discuss, Christ's saying 'If ye forgive men their trespasses your heavenly Father will also forgive you' (Matthew 6:14).

49

A man might hold that *anybody* – Jesus' contemporaries, medieval theologians, our contemporaries – simply misunderstand these words if they take them to refer to a 'transcendent' personal being who would reward our forgiving those who have trespassed against us by forgiving us our trespasses against *him*. If this view is taken, an 'interpretation' will attempt to cut through centuries of misinterpretation to the actual meaning Jesus intended his words to have for those who heard them. This, I think, is the Pelzs' approach.

But other writers (of whom van Buren is an example) stress that Jesus himself was obliged to express himself in the thought-forms of the culture in which he found himself, and that if we are to find the enduring meaning of his words for us in *our* 'thought-world', it is not enough to get back to what Jesus *actually meant*. Living within a 'supernatural' world-view, Jesus naturally meant to speak about a 'supernatural' God, and a 'supernatural' Heaven and Hell. However, these writers go on to argue, there is something in Jesus' words which remains true even when our 'supernatural' beliefs have gone: and it is that which is to be isolated and expressed in contemporary terms.

It would, I suppose, be possible for someone who took the second view to hold that we modern people had escaped from all the world-views or conceptual frameworks which distorted the perception of our predecessors, and that from our vantage point we were able to see where prevailing thought-forms had determined the formulation of doctrines in times past, and able therefore to express their 'essence' in terms which would continue to be valid forever.

In this case however we should have to argue convincingly against the strong presumption that if we consider every other age to be structured by a prevailing world-view we must consider our own age to be similarly placed. And indeed all the important writers (as far as my knowledge goes) who argue that the original formulation of Christian doctrine was subject to the conceptual framework obtaining at the time admit also that what *we* say and write in modern times is structured in an exactly parallel way. Conceptual frameworks may differ from age to age, but every age has one. It is this version of the second enterprise of 'interpretation' that we shall therefore consider.

The first enterprise – that of getting at what someone, or someone's words, actually meant – is much the less perplexing of the two. Practically, it may sometimes be a very difficult business; and of course it has its own philosophical difficulties. Yet its possibility is a presupposition of all our knowledge about the past which relies on written documents.

The distinction upon which the second enterprise relies is succinctly expressed in words of Pope John XXIII: 'The substance of the ancient doctrine . . . is one thing; its formulation is quite another' (quoted by Mascall, [1] p. 1). It is a distinction, however, that involves great difficulty.

First there is the huge threat which faces every extreme relativist: he is sawing away at the branch on which he is sitting. In the present case, it is claimed that we can never express a doctrine in a form of words which will be always true, since to express it at all we must express it in terms belonging to an essentially temporary 'thought-world'. The difficulty is, of course, that this claim is *itself* one of the things that is couched in terms belonging to a 'thought-world': and so ex hypothesi cannot be unchangingly true.

A second highly unsatisfactory feature of the position we are considering, closely connected with the point just raised, is the oddity of holding that the 'eternal truth' or the 'essence' of a doctrine can never be stated. Every valid doctrine embodies an essential truth, it is claimed, but when we ask what that essential truth is we are told it cannot be stated. Mascall goes some way towards acknowledging this difficulty when he says: 'Granted that the formulations may legitimately differ, how can we specify and recognise the substance? Clearly, not by laying down some unalterable form of words, for this would be simply an additional formulation' (Mascall, [1] p. 36).

But in this case, how can postulating a distinction between 'essence' and 'formulation' or between 'eternal truth' and 'transient expression' be of any use? The point of introducing it must be to explain how it is possible to distinguish legitimately an acceptable formulation of Christian doctrine from an invalid one. Yet if no one can say what the essence of a doctrine is how can we have good grounds for saying *this* formulation catches it while *that* one does not?

Rather than leave this as a purely rhetorical question, let us consider the specific answer that Mascall has developed for it. It is as well that this writer in particular attempts an answer since he is one who repeatedly and with a great show of certi-

51

tude denounces one New Theologian after another for purveying something *other* than Christianity, and who thus places great weight on the possibility of sorting, in his own terminology, 'substance' from 'formulation'.

In passing it is perhaps interesting to notice that Mascall, as a representative of the theological 'right', recognises no less than the radical that there is a need to re-express the 'permanent truths' of Christianity in the temporary 'thought-forms' of successive generations. At the very outset of 'The Secularization of Christianity,' it is written that 'One of the most imperative duties with which the Christian theologian is confronted is that of relating the revealed datum of Christian truth, final, absolute and fundamentally permanent as he must by his Christian commitment believe it to be, to the essentially incomplete, relative and constantly changing intellectual framework of the world in which he lives' (Mascall, [1] p. 1). Thus does Mascall assert his 'Yes' to the *kind* of project van Buren and the others have been engaged on – even though the rest of his book is devoted to pronouncing his '*but*'.

Mascall's account of how we are to distinguish valid interpretation from invalid is based on the bold conviction that 'the truth itself (the "substance of the doctrine" as distinct from its "formulation") exists in its fullness in the mind of Christ . . .'; it exists there '. . . not as a set of propositions explored by the discursive reason but as one totally apprehended object of the intellect, possessed in all its fullness in one supreme contemplative act' (Mascall, [1] p. 38). How then is the theologian to apprise himself of this truth? In so far as he is able to at all, Mascall explains that the theologian is to form 'a deliberate habit of loyal submission to Christian tradition . . .' (Mascall, [1] p. 36). For one thing 'he must and can be convinced of is the truth of the great Christian tradition . . .' (Mascall, [1] p. 38). Having asserted this in uncompromising terms, Mascall nevertheless feels able to assert also that the poor theologian 'may at times have a painful [but, it is implied, justified] suspicion that the tradition, as it has been presented to him, is, in this or the other respect, distorted, unbalanced, stunted, fossilised, forgetful of its own past achievements or insensitive to the needs and demands of the contemporary world'. And when this is so, 'he will . . . make his own contribution to the common inheritance . . .' (Mascall, [1] pp. 37–8). 'It is in this way',

Mascall concludes with satisfaction, 'that I would solve the problem of the relation between the immutable substance of Christian doctrine and the mutability and unfinished character of its verbal expression' (Mascall, [1] pp. 38–9).

Is this 'solution' of Mascall's acceptable? Surely not. For it derives any plausibility it has from an equivocation over the phrase 'the Christian tradition'.

First, Mascall sometimes means by it something that we can refer to here and now. It is to this that the theologian is required to turn in submission – 'the great body of Christian thought' (Mascall, [1] p. 37), as embodied, presumably, in the great accumulated mass of classical theological writings regarded by the orthodox as orthodox. It is in *this* sense (and this sense only) that the Christian tradition could provide a practical criterion for distinguishing 'substance' from 'formulation'.

But Mascall also used the phrase to refer to 'the truth itself' – the 'substance of the doctrine' as it is alleged to exist 'in the mind of Christ'. 'The Christian tradition' in this second sense refers, in other words, exclusively to what is *true* in 'the Christian tradition' in the first sense. It is the second sense alone which is compatible with Mascall's saying that the theologian can be convinced of the truth of the tradition 'even when he is in the humiliating position of not being sure that he *or anyone else* [my italics] has yet adequately understood its content or seen it in its true proportions' (Mascall, [1] p. 38).

But *this* sense of tradition provides no court of appeal capable of settling what is 'immutable' in Christian doctrine and what is not. If the 'tradition' is to be understood as residing 'in the mind of Christ' it is, for the present at least, not available for *public* consultation.

So out of Mascall's cunningly constructed statement a straightforward question arises: Can the Christian tradition sometimes be in error? In the first sense of 'Christian tradition', it can be; in that case it cannot act as a sure criterion for distinguishing truth from error, or substance from formulation. In the second sense of 'Christian tradition' it cannot be in error: but in this case it is irretrievably beyond the pale, of no help whatever in making our present distinctions. Our problem of telling substance from formulation remains.

Can we draw any conclusions from this brief discussion of 'interpretation'? As regards the first, less problematic, enterprise

53

we distinguished, it may be worth remarking that in such a project great importance will attach to linguistic and cultural study of the language and environment of the writings to be 'interpreted'. Theological, philosophical or even religious insights will not themselves be enough.

Where writers deny that it is the first of the projects we have distinguished which engages them, then I think it must be their responsibility to explain what exactly they are attempting to do. The one account of this kind which we *did* examine – the one which traded on a distinction between 'essence' and 'formulation' – we found, I think, unsatisfactory. If there are others, they will have to be brought forward.

It is true, of course, that the issue of distinguishing valid from invalid interpretation is less crucial for the typical radical than it is for the conservative. For traditionally at least (and see Geach's chapter 'On Worshipping the Right God' in 'God and the Soul' for evidence that the tradition is a living one) it mattered enormously that it was *Christianity* in which a man believed – an approximation would not serve. To believe the truth was to be saved; to fall into heresy, damnation.

Lacking (as a rule) these curious epistemological convictions, the radical, and the uncommitted person too, finds less pressing the need to secure the distinction in question, and thus typically fails to face up to the explicit problem of 'the development of doctrine' to which we have heard the conservative (in the person of Mascall) address himself.

Nevertheless, it is also true that the radical is to be found repeatedly attempting to reconcile his views with those of traditional Christianity, without, as far as my knowledge goes, making any serious attempt to make clear what criteria such 'reconciliations' are appealing to. At least almost always – in van Buren, in Cox, in the Pelzs, for example – one is left to consult one's intuitions: though sometimes, one must confess, as in the 'translation' of Cox's we quoted at the beginning of this discussion, one's intuitions seem more than enough.

('Christianity and Paradox', p. 195). He explains carefully what he means by this (and we are reminded strongly of Braithwaite): 'We could describe as "religious" any set of attitudes and beliefs that satisfies three conditions. First, the believer commits himself to a pattern of ethical behaviour. This way of life is simply decided for as an ultimate moral choice. . . . [Second], what will distinguish religious from moral language is that religious discourse provides a tightly cohering extended parable or myth that vividly expresses the way of life chosen, and inspires the believer to implement it in practice. Third, the parable and its associated pattern of behaviour legislate not for any *fraction* of the believer's life, but for every aspect of it' (Hepburn, p. 195).

Hepburn then points out that all three conditions can be fulfilled by a set of attitudes and beliefs which make no reference to 'the Supernatural', so that the sceptic, the man who 'cannot conscientiously believe in God as the New Testament depicts him' (Hepburn, p. 197), can nevertheless retain his religious orientation of mind: he can be seen as 'perpetually in quest of the most satisfactory set of parables to sum up his moral decisions'. Hepburn goes on: 'The field from which he will glean material is indefinitely large. . . . He may stock his armoury of symbols from such novels as Orwell's 'Animal Farm', and Koestler's 'Darkness at Noon'; from Dostoievsky's 'The Idiot', from Bunyan and from Spenser, promiscuously; from Euripides in 'The Bacchae'. Upon each encounter with these and the like myth-makers something will be taken, something rejected; the moral struggle seen more sharply through the lens of the new parable. . . . It is a task in which imagination cooperates intimately with moral judgment – discriminating, amending, adapting, in order to build up an image of the best way of life and the best way of capturing it, in myth, parable and symbol. . . . To organize one's life in this way', Hepburn concludes, 'would I think be admitted by some people as a genuinely religious activity' (Hepburn, pp. 197–8).

In appraising these views, we must begin by registering our surprise that so seasoned a campaigner as Hepburn should have chanced his arm with a *definition* – and of 'religion' of all things! To compile a list of collectively sufficient conditions for the application of a term (in this case 'religious') is always thankless task, and often surely an impossible one. As it stand

3 Living without 'The Beyond'

'I think having no religion makes one feel that nothing matters.'

Fleur, in Galsworthy's 'A Modern Comedy'

What I claim to be the loss of the concept of the supernatural, then, has had, as one would expect, large implications for the 'supernatural' religion we know as Christianity, and we have looked at some attempts that have been made to take account of them. But does 'the Supernatural's' demise have even more general implications?

Some people have thought, for example, that religion of any kind is impossible without the notion of the supernatural (Mr T. S. Eliot is one of these – see the quotation at the head of Chapter 2 above); many have felt, perhaps merely putting this same fear in a different way, that the loss of 'the Supernatural' would render morality empty and destroy the very meaning of life.

These questions are raised in an interesting way in the writings of Ronald Hepburn. Among writers who have sympathies with Christianity, Hepburn occupies an unusual position. On his one hand stand those who have accepted the loss of the concept of the supernatural and have attempted to recast Christianity in a 'non-supernatural' mould, while on his other stand the conservatives who declare such a recasting to be unnecessary and in any case impossible. Hepburn himself sees things of great value in Christianity but at the same time insists that it cannot survive the difficulties we have referred to. His suggestion is therefore that in losing its 'supernatural' reference Christianity does indeed lose its identity, but that what remains (when this loss has occurred) may still be of considerable value: it is not Christianity but it is still worth having.

1 Hepburn's 'religious orientation'

What remains, Hepburn is primarily concerned to argue, is the possibility of possessing a 'religious orientation of mind

Hepburn's self-confessed 'definition' allows as a 'religion' a political ideology like Communism, a philosophical outlook like Existentialism as well as the principles of the man who conducts his life in the light of de Sade's 'Justine'. There is clearly something, if not everything, wrong with calling these 'religions': for one thing (as regards the first two cases), 'religion' is frequently what the communist or the existentialist is himself most anxious to denounce.

Moreover, although it does not strictly count against Hepburn's explicit claim to be putting forward collectively *sufficient* conditions for the application of 'religious', it is interesting to realise that should they be thought of as *necessary* conditions too (does Hepburn hint at this?) Christianity itself would not qualify as a religion. For 'the story that backs up the morality' in Christianity, if we can speak in such terms, is allegedly *factual*, not mythical or parabolic. As Hepburn himself says, '. . . an account of religion in terms of a moral way of life backed up by parable fails [i.e. is not adequate] as a description of Christianity . . .' (Hepburn, p. 194); and so the second condition (conceived of as *necessary*) he puts forward for the application of 'religious' is not fulfilled.

As I have already (above, p. 5) had occasion to indicate, however, the obligation to offer a definition of the kind Hepburn thinks of himself as presenting here arises only as a consequence of accepting a particular theory of general terms – the theory that implies that all individuals which fall properly under a general term (e.g. 'religion') must have some feature or features common and peculiar to them. For independent reasons, this theory is not very satisfactory; and alternatives to it have been put forward. It is not easy to say anything that is at once brief and worthwhile on this difficult issue, but since I invoke the possibility of such an alternative more than once in the course of this essay, I feel duty bound to digress briefly upon it.

The name that is usually associated with the project of developing an alternative view to what we earlier (above, p. 5) called the 'common and peculiar features' view is that of Wittgenstein, and we can use his phrase for the kind of approach he sketched – the approach which depends on the notion of 'family resemblance'.

Perhaps what is distinctive about a family resemblance view

57

can be put very crudely like this. Consider four individual things. The 'common and peculiar features' theory would insist that if all four are to be subsumed under a common term, one or more features must be shared by all of them. If we give features letters, we might represent our four individuals thus:

1. a b c .   .   .
2. a d e .   .   .
3. a f g .   .   .
4. a h i .   .   .

Here the common feature a would allow all four individuals to be subsumed under a general term. But consider a second set of four individuals with no such common feature:

5. a b c .   .   .
6. b c d .   .   .
7. c d e .   .   .
8. d e f .   .   .

In this case individuals 5 and 8 have nothing in common – except their both having things in common with individuals 6 and 7: and it is this relationship which justifies, so it is argued on a 'family resemblance' view, subsuming 5 and 8 under the same general term.

These contrasting pictures however are no more than visual aids. They involve treating the notion of a feature as though a definite set were possessed by each individual thing, whereas in fact everything has an unlimited number of features: or perhaps it might be even more correct to say that features of things (like 'things' as such themselves) cannot be counted as such at all.

Moreover, the picture I have presented gives no hint as to how an ordinary resemblance is to be distinguished from a resemblance which justifies the application of a single common term. Things often bear resemblances to one another – have features in common: how is one to tell when the resemblance is, as the name of the theory puts it, a *family* resemblance?

The notion of a type or paradigm to some extent eases these difficulties, as William Whewell tried to urge when he debated what was fundamentally the same issue as ours with J. S. Mill. The context in their case was explicitly biological classification, with Mill on the one hand holding that for the same common name to be applied to a set of individuals they had to share a common characteristic, and Whewell on the other arguing that what was necessary was rather their all being related to a

58

common *type* (see J. S. Mill, 'System of Logic', bk 4, ch. 7, and W. Whewell, 'Philosophy of the Inductive Sciences, bk viii, chs i and ii).

Whewell explains what he means by this: 'A type is an example of any class, for instance, a species, or a genus, which is considered as eminently possessing the characters of the class' (Whewell, p. 476). Thus, for him 'the class is steadily fixed, though not precisely limited: it is given, though not circumscribed; it is determined, not by a boundary line without, but by a central point within; not by what it strictly excludes, but by what it eminently includes; by an example, not by a precept; in short, instead of Definition we have a Type for our director' (Whewell, p. 476).

Much more recently, M. A. Simon has attempted to develop in precise terms this notion of a paradigm as providing an answer to the question (with which he labels his article) 'When is a resemblance a family resemblance?' ('Mind', 1969).

If I cite a particular feature of a thing as making it a thing of a certain sort (for example, if I say that inventing spoonerisms is a game 'because it has the element of amusement' (Simon, p. 411)), it can only be, in Simon's view, because there is or is conceived to be a *paradigm* which possesses that feature. A list of features may, on this view, be drawn up such that at least one feature on the list must be possessed by a thing if it is to fall in the category in question. But the list defines the *paradigm*: it does not specify a set of features common and peculiar to all the things that can be said to be things of the sort in question. Putting it in terms of Wittgenstein's example of a game, Simon writes: 'the point is not that there is no set of features that properly constitutes anything that possesses them as a game, but rather that this set of "essential" features defines not a game but merely a paradigm case of a game' (Simon, p. 413).

Thus, on this theory, it is not necessary for two things to have a common feature in order to be subsumed under the same common term: they may be so subsumed in virtue of each having paradigmatic features which differ and yet belong to the same paradigm.

Simon's account is brief, and partly inadequate for this reason. To raise again my difficulty with the notion of a feature, why cannot we say that on Simon's view, *pace* himself, things of the same sort have to have at least one feature in common,

59

namely that of having a paradigmatic feature in common with the same paradigm? As it stands, that is to say, the notion of a feature is too vague.

But more basically perhaps I wonder whether Simon is right to rule out the possibility of a thing being atypical of its kind in *every* respect. Would it not be possible for a completely atypical thing to be classed as belonging to a kind in virtue of its having much in common with a thing that was *itself* almost as atypical, but which belonged to the kind in virtue of having things in common with individuals which were a little less atypical – and so on?

Neither these nor any other criticisms can be taken further here. But in spite of them, I think we have said enough to establish that the 'common and peculiar features' theory of general terms is not the only contender in the field, and we shall proceed on this basis. In the present context we shall be prepared, that is to say, to define 'religion' by referring to features typical of it, without sharing Hepburn's assumption that such features must be 'common and peculiar'.

Regarded, less pedantically perhaps, as a definition of *this* kind, that is, as a list of features *typical* of religions or religious activities, Hepburn's account is still unsatisfactory. It is to be criticised both for the important things it neglects and for the intellectualist emphasis of what it includes. Take Hepburn's first point: a religious believer, we take him to say, typically 'decides upon a way of life' as an ultimate moral choice: yet such a choice can only be available in a culture if such there be where there is more than one 'way of life', and even there, it can only be open to those who for some reason become conscious that there is a choice to be made – even in a culture like ours, surely most of us unreflectingly follow the crowd accident has placed us in.

Besides the choice of an all-embracing moral code, Hepburn lists only the backing such a code receives in a religion from parable and myth. If it is typical religions we are talking about, however, we had better add that what *we* are calling parable and myth is typically regarded by the religious believers themselves as fact. Typically, religious people believe distinctive things about the universe: they believe it to be peopled with gods, haunted by spirits; and the man who uses religious words like 'god' and 'spirit' *only* in stories, even if they are high-grade

60

stories like myths and parables, is not a typical man of religion.

One very important matter not referred to in Hepburn's definition is the element of *worship* – which many people have regarded as central to religion. (We shall have to return to it shortly.) Nor does he mention rites and ritual, nor the role of a class of people of special status – a priesthood or the like, nor belief in some kind of existence for the individual besides his existence here and now. Yet all these seem typical of religion.

These points are mentioned, however, not in order to argue that Hepburn's 'religious orientation' is not religious at all, but to stress the fact that it is far from being a *typical* case of religion.

The significance of the issue Hepburn is arguing about here – that is, roughly, the issue of whether searching for the most satisfactory set of parables to sum up one's moral decisions (Hepburn, p. 197) can properly be regarded as a *religious* activity – is, however, dubious. What does it matter whether we agree to call it 'religious'? We know that Hepburn is recommending it as a way of life; and we can realise with reflection that as a way of life it will lack many of the elements to be found in a *typically* religious way of life: what more is there to discuss?

2 The numinous

One of the things that play a large part in a typical religion, we have already said, is *worship*. Is the possibility of worship inextricably tied up with the notion of the supernatural, or can we retain the former without the latter?

Hepburn himself touches on a closely related question when he asks whether a secular person could enjoy the possibility of experiencing what has come to be called 'numinous experience'.

By this is meant the allegedly ineffable feeling, compounded of awe, wonder, fascination, dread, a sense of strangeness, terror and other elements, which is felt by some people in holy places, by others, sometimes, in the face of nature, and imaginatively by many of us (in its crudest form) when we think of ourselves as seeing a ghost. According to its most eminent theoretician, Rudolf Otto, the numinous experience, when 'raised to its highest power' becomes the *mystical* experience. Kenneth

Grahame has left a memorable picture of what the experience involves in chapter vii of 'The Wind in the Willows'. Mole and Rat have been led to an island by the fascinating pipe music:

'This is the place of my song-dream, the place the music played to me', whispered the Rat, as if in a trance. 'Here, in this holy place, here if anywhere, surely we shall find Him!'

Then suddenly the Mole felt a great Awe fall upon him, an awe that turned his muscles to water, bowed his head, and rooted his feet to the ground. It was no panic terror – indeed he felt wonderfully at peace and happy – but it was an awe that smote him and held him and, without seeing, he knew it could only mean that some august Presence was very, very near. With difficulty he turned to look for his friend, and saw him at his side, cowed, stricken, and trembling violently. . . . Perhaps he would never have dared to raise his eyes, but that . . . the call and the summons seemed still dominant and imperious. . . . Trembling he obeyed, and raised his humble head; and then . . . he looked in the very eyes of the Friend and Helper . . . and . . . as he looked, he lived, and still, as he lived, he wondered.

'Rat!' he found breath to whisper, shaking. 'Are you afraid?'

'Afraid?' murmured the Rat, his eyes shining with unutterable love. 'Afraid! of Him. O, never, never! And yet – and yet – O, Mole, I am afraid!'

Then the two animals, crouching to the earth, bowed their heads and did worship.

In his last sentence Grahame interestingly brings out the connection between experiencing the numinous and worshipping, to which we shall have to return. But first we must consider Hepburn's problem: whether numinous experiences can be had by the secular man.

The difficulty, as Hepburn sees it, is that numinous experiences are often (at least) thought of by the people who have them to be revelations of a 'transcendent' or 'supernatural' reality. If the latter notions are rejected, therefore, the continued 'availability' of such experiences is, thinks Hepburn, put in doubt.

His own view is, however, that all that is necessary in order

62

for them to be experienced by the sceptic is for the latter to be prepared to 'reinterpret' them along 'non-supernatural' lines. The sceptic would, it is true, be quite unable to regard numinous experience as a revelation of a 'transcendent' reality; but it *would* be possible for him to think of nature as being able to assume a 'quasi-personal hue' from time to time – a 'hue' recognised in the numinous experience (Hepburn, pp. 207–8). Reinterpreted in some such way, Hepburn thus concludes that the numinous experience 'remains available' to the sceptic.

First I may remark that I find Hepburn's use of 'available' in this connection a little curious: he speaks as though it would be sensible to suppose that one could set one's heart on having a numinous experience only to discover that because of one's metaphysical beliefs none was, after all, to be had.

More importantly – though this is a connected point – we must notice Hepburn's explicit presupposition that 'sense of the numinous does not bring with it its own interpretation' (Hepburn, p. 206). He believes that it is possible to distinguish between the numinous experience 'in itself', in other words, and the interpretation that is imposed upon it, which is, we are told, 'the product of reflection about the experience and of the decision about what thought-model will distort it least' (Hepburn, p. 206).

This seems to me to be almost straightforwardly wrong. If one turns to the accounts of numinous experiences in William James or W. T. Stace's book 'Mysticism and Philosophy' for example, the notion of the experients having their experiences and then reflecting for a bit and finally deciding on the 'thought-model' which will 'least distort' what they have just gone through seems wholly inappropriate. Their accounts instead show boundless confidence in the experience and what it revealed to them (or as a third party should say, what they thought it revealed to them). There is utter conviction, unshakeable certainty: and absolutely nothing of the tentativeness and caution which Hepburn's picture suggests.

W. T. Stace has defended a thesis similar to Hepburn's, however, which evades the particular difficulty we have raised. Stace's thesis explicitly concerns *mystical* experiences, but if we accept for a moment what is, as I have already indicated, the orthodoxy that numinous experiences are a species of mystical experience we can regard it as relevant to our present problem.

63

Stace evades our objection simply by omitting any mention of the 'reflection' followed by a 'decision' about the appropriateness of 'thought-models' which Hepburn insists on. But about the validity of a distinction between the mystical experience and its interpretation Stace agrees. His view is that there is one basic experience common to all mysticism wherever and whenever it occurs, namely, 'an awareness of *Unity*'. The different accounts we have of the phenomenon from the different religious traditions merely reflect the different interpretations that have been put upon experiences that are 'phenomenologically' (Stace, p. 29) the same.

Even without the temporal element involved in Hepburn's formulation, the attempt to distinguish 'experience' from 'interpretation' in this context seems to me to be misguided. Suppose three of us dream about a fabulous monster. I describe mine as a large animal having a coat of white wool; you describe yours as a lugubrious beast with udders; he describes his as a scaly amphibian. A mutual acquaintance of patience listens to our accounts and upon their conclusion delivers himself of this remarkable judgement: 'I can see that despite the superficial differences of your accounts, all of you in fact had the same dream experience; you, dear friend, interpreted what you saw as having a white coat because you are a shepherd; you, as having udders because you are a cowherd; and you, as being scaly and amphibious since you are a fisherman. But underneath these different descriptions it is plain there runs a single experience common to you all.'

Such a claim would be puzzling. How would we distinguish between on the one hand having the same experience as another man, but interpreting it differently, and on the other having a different experience from his? I do not see how we could – either in this case or in the one in which Stace and Hepburn are interested. And if we could not, then surely Stace's and Hepburn's attempted distinction cannot be maintained.

We cannot therefore accept the possibility of the sceptic interpreting in a 'non-supernatural' way an experience which a religious person would interpret in a 'supernatural' way. On the other hand it is easy to envisage these two people having experiences which are alike in certain respects, but which one describes in terms which involve reference to 'supernatural' things but which the other describes in terms which make no such reference.

Indeed, enough interesting actual cases of this kind are to be found in Stace, for example, for envisaging to be unnecessary. Many people are on record as having had experiences similar in many, and more or less specifiable, ways to the religious experience of the numinous which they nevertheless have described in non-religious (and 'non-supernatural') terms. Here is one of them:

> Suddenly every object in my field of vision took on a curious and intense kind of existence of its own; that is, everything appeared to have an 'inside' – to exist as I existed, having inwardness, a kind of individual life, and every object, seen under this aspect, appeared exceedingly beautiful. . . . Everything was *urgent* with life. . . . All things seemed to glow with a light that came from within them. . . . I experienced a complete certainty that at that moment I saw things as they really were, and I was filled with grief at the realization of the real situation of human beings, living continuously in the midst of all this without being aware of it. (Quoted by Stace from a personal informant, pp. 70–2)

Perhaps it was only the possibility of this kind of experience that Hepburn wished to establish: if so we cede it gladly.

Yet some brief remarks suggest that he may read into his conclusion more than this. On page 208 he apparently takes himself to have established the possibility of a sceptic enjoying a kind of nature mysticism. This we can accept. Indeed in our view it needs no establishing, since it is usually acknowledged that the non-supernaturalist mystical experience of nature which we have just illustrated happens not infrequently. But he goes on to allow himself to conclude from this that nature 'lends itself' to this kind of experience:

> It is . . . a matter for wonderment that nature should *lend* itself as it does to these human activities, should be so malleable to our imagination, that it should "take" our projections, and (from sometimes unpromising material!) make something so rich and strange out of them. This is a fact of importance about nature itself – one of the many

reasons against thinking of it as destructive of, or at least hostile to, all value. (Hepburn, p. 208)

But this is surely loose thinking. Are we to say that the drunkard's pink rats 'lend themselves' to the sot's imagination? This can only be a colourful way of saying something about the drunkard's *imagination*, not about pink rats.

Having admitted, though, that 'nature mysticism' seems possible among those who have no 'supernaturalist' faith, we must at least query the identification in Hepburn, and in the foregoing, between this kind of experience and experience of the *numinous*. This comes out clearly if the passage from 'The Wind in the Willows' is compared with the report of a sceptic's 'mystical' experience I quoted from W. T. Stace. The distinctive feelings of dread and strangeness, stressed by Grahame in the former, do not figure in the latter. Or we might measure the report in Stace against the classic analysis of the numinous experience by Otto. He finds that it is characterised by a feeling of *awe*, of being utterly *overpowered*, and of *energy* or urgency; there is, he says, a profound sense of *stupor* and, finally, a feeling of *fascination* (Otto, 'The Idea of the Holy, pp. 24–5).

Of these 'feeling-elements' as Otto calls them, there seems in particular to have been no sense of 'being overpowered' in the sceptic's experience, and this perhaps suggests one of the important differences between the sceptic and the supernaturalist in this respect. The former cannot regard the world as *personal* in the way that the latter can. He cannot think of himself as being 'overpowered' by what his experience reveals, since to be overpowered is to have one's will swept aside by another, and to believe nature to embody a 'will' or 'wills' is precisely *not* to be a sceptic (in the present sense).

Because the non-supernaturalist cannot regard nature or inanimate objects as personal therefore (without ceasing to be a non-supernaturalist) it seems that there may be difficulties after all in his having an experience properly described as numinous. It seems implicit in Otto's account, for example, that the numinous object of an experience has to be regarded as personal by the experient if it is to qualify as a 'numinous' object.

The same is true, I think, of objects of *worship*: they must be regarded as personal. Many people, of course, seem to worship what we should call inanimate things: but this shows, I suggest, that they themselves do not share our view of the things they are worshipping: for them, the objects are 'personal'.

The point here perhaps emerges most clearly when we consider certain degenerate uses of 'worship'. A miser might be said to 'worship' his gold, a fetishist to 'worship', say, a fur kaross. We would mean, in the latter case for example, that his mind is constantly preoccupied with the fetish object, that he always handles it with great and loving care, that he envisages its loss as the worst of horrors. But there is no question in such a case of putting the interests of this thing he 'worships' above his own; there is no question of his submitting himself to its will. It is not regarded as *having* any interests, as having a 'will': it is not regarded as being a person. And this is the reason, I suggest, for our practice (at least when we are being strict) of enclosing 'worship' in such cases within inverted commas. This kind of fetishism is not a case of worship in a full sense, because the object is throughout regarded as an inanimate object.

If it is necessary for the object of worship to be personal, perhaps the non-supernaturalist may find satisfactory objects in the people around him? Often, certainly, we speak of one person 'worshipping' another. In such cases the subordination of interest and the submission of will we spoke of above are both possible, and both typically occur. Nevertheless, the inverted commas remain round 'worship', I think, so long as the devotee regards the object of his feeling as 'just' a person, even though an extraordinary one. To be said to worship him or her in a literal sense, he would surely have to regard him or her as essentially different from himself, as belonging to 'a different order of being'.

To the man who believes there is only one 'order of being' – i.e. to the non-supernaturalist – worship, and even numinous experience, in a full sense would seem therefore to be impossible. For we have just suggested that (natural) persons cannot serve as objects of worship, properly conceived; and moreover, as we have also argued, objects of worship have to be *at least* personal, even if they have to be more than personal. And since the non-supernaturalist cannot regard things other than human beings as personal and remain a non-supernaturalist, we can only conclude that the possibility of worship is not open to him.

The question of whether the loss of 'the Supernatural' undermines morality seems to me to need less discussion. On

67

the one hand that such a development is likely to affect people's judgement as to how they should conduct themselves need hardly be argued for; while on the other, the claim that morality at all is only possible alongside a belief in 'God' or 'the world to come' seems pretty clearly untenable. The argument that the threat of 'supernatural' sanctions can alone provide a reason for eschewing self-interest has only to be stated to be silenced: for the one thing a man is *not* doing if he performs an act in order to secure some future benefit for himself is acting unselfishly.

3 *The meaning of life*

The secular man need not fear for his morality. But can he regard life as *meaningful*? Can he have a positive answer to the question: What is the meaning of life? This is a matter which calls for a more sustained enquiry.

(a) *Setting life within a context*

Sometimes in asking for 'the meaning of life' a man takes himself to be asking about the *purpose* of life: the one phrase is thought of as synonymous with the other. The issues, on this interpretation, are relatively straightforward. As Kurt Baier points out in his businesslike lecture on 'The Meaning of Life', a thing can be said to have a purpose in either of two senses: 'In the first and basic sense, purpose is normally attributed only to persons or their behaviour as in 'Did you have a purpose in leaving the ignition on?' In the second sense, purpose is normally attributed only to things [that are not agents], as in 'What is the purpose of that gadget you installed in the workshop?' (Baier, p. 19).

If we ask about the purpose of life, in a straightforward sense, we cannot be asking about the purpose 'life' entertains as an agent; for if we are non-supernaturalists, we can hardly regard life as being an agent at all. Rather, we must be asking about purpose in Baier's second sense. We are asking about the purpose *behind* life, about the purpose life was designed to fulfil.

It is perfectly clear, though, that in this sense having a purpose implies the activity of a 'purposer'. If we ask: What is the

68

purpose of a car's hooter? we are implying that the hooter was incorporated into the car's design by an engineer who was wanting it to do some job. Its purpose, we may say, is to provide the driver with a way of giving audible warning of approach. Or we could turn this around a little and say that the designer incorporated a hooter into the motor car *with the purpose* of enabling audible warning of approach to be given. Similarly, in saying that the purpose of a certain orifice is to allow lubrication I can be understood as saying that the hole was designed into the apparatus with the purpose of facilitating lubrication.

To speak of a thing having a purpose, therefore, implies either that it is itself an agent or that there is an agent behind it conferring purpose upon it. In either case, the non-supernaturalist must deny that life has a purpose. He could not regard life as itself a 'purposer', and being unable to give a sense to 'supernatural' agents, could see no sense in asking for what purpose life had been devised.

To regard the question: What is the meaning of life? as asking: 'What is the purpose of life? is only one possibility, however. Another would be to regard it as asking for life to be related to its 'context', for an account of the role life plays in the 'whole' to which it belongs.

Citing purposes is one way of relating a thing to its context: in explaining the purpose of a car hooter one is explaining the part it plays in the general business of safe driving. But there are others which do not involve reference to purposes. Thus a biological innocent may wonder about the point of the heart; and may be told that it is there to pump the blood round. Although he may equally well have expressed himself by asking: What's the purpose of the heart? or: What's the heart for? he is not really asking about purposes in the sense we have been considering so far. He is asking about the *function* of the heart. He wants to know what part it plays in the human body as a whole. He wants the heart, in the phrase we used above, *related to its context*.

Similarly, sociologists have been much occupied with the question: What is the point (or meaning) of religion? in the sense that this question asks about the *function* that the institution of religion fulfils in human society. Here human society is taken to be the 'whole', and in asking about the point of religion we are asking for it to be related to this whole.

And so, it may be, with 'the meaning of life'. When we ask

69

what this meaning is we may be asking for life to be related to the whole of which, we may think, it is but a part.

This comes out clearly, I think, when we look at some of the answers which supernaturalists from time to time have given to it. Putting it a trifle colourfully, perhaps, we may imagine a supernaturalist explaining that the point of life is to act as an aperitif to the eternal banquet, which can only begin once our glasses have been drained. Or it might be said that the point of life is to be a kind of sixth-form course, leading, for those who make the grade, to a place in the divine University. Yet another view might be that life is the first scene in a large drama devised by some cosmic tragedian. These views and of course many others are possible. They all relate life to a 'whole' that is greater than life: each relates life to a wider context. But of course they are all views which presuppose a supernaturalist outlook. They presuppose belief in 'a world to come', in existence going on 'beyond the grave', of the natural order being included within and as part of the 'supernatural' or 'eternal' order.

Our question has to be, however: What if we deny these beliefs? Can those of us who believe that this world is the only world 'relate life to a wider context'? One way of doing this, if we took the word 'life' very literally, would be to show the place of human life in what we know of the general scheme of evolution: to show how human life evolved out of animal life, how the whole of animate life arose out of the inanimate world, how that world relates to other bodies in the universe. This would be to set human life, and life in general, within a wider context and thus to show it to have a 'point'.

(b) *The meaning of it all*

Yet such an answer, one suspects, would do nothing to satisfy anyone who had bothered to raise the large question in the first place. In asking: What is the meaning of life? it may well be said, the sense of 'life' is not to be taken so narrowly. What is really being asked about is the meaning of the whole of existence as human beings encounter it. We must imagine the man who asks it reflecting on everything that he has come across in his life, on the whole universe as it presents itself to him, and asking: What does it all mean? Here he is not asking about human life literally understood, and will not be satisfied with talk of cosmic and organic evolution: he is asking about *everything* – evolution included.

But if this is the question, what sort of an answer can the secular man give? For him, the universe we know is all that there is: there is nothing beyond it to which he can refer, no context wider than the universe to which the universe can be related. If the demand to be told the meaning of life is a demand to have the whole of existence as we know it related to a wider context, it is a demand which the secular man cannot meet.

Yet still another interpretation is possible. In 'The Meanings of the Questions of Life' John Wisdom draws our attention to a question we may ask after seeing a difficult play. Sometimes, he says 'even when we have seen and heard a play from the beginning to the end' we are puzzled and ask 'what does the whole thing mean [?] In this case we are not asking what came before or what came after, we are not asking about anything outside the play itself. . . . Our words express a wish to grasp the character, the significance of the whole play. They are a confession that we have not yet done this and they are a request for help in doing it. Is the play a tragedy, a comedy or a tale told by an idiot? The pattern of it is so complex, so bewildering, our grasp of it still so inadequate, that we don't know what to say, still less whether to call it good or bad.' In a similar way, Wisdom is suggesting 'with the words "what is the meaning of it all?" we are trying to find the order in the drama of Time' (Wisdom, [7] pp. 40–1).

Although the example of play appreciation taken here may do perfectly well the job Wisdom wanted it to do, it is worth remarking, I think, how limited that job is. What it shows, and all it shows, is that there *are* cases in which we are prepared to talk of 'the meaning' of a thing without referring to something beyond itself.

Like the conclusion of our earlier discussion about purposes – that in *some* areas we were prepared to speak of 'the meaning' of a thing even though purposes were not involved – our present finding is wholly negative. Both counter possible objections, but help us hardly at all with the positive task of understanding what might be meant by speaking of the 'meaning of life' within a conceptual framework which lacks the concept of the supernatural.

It might be thought, even by himself, that Wisdom's play case does more than provide a counterinstance to the objection that you can only speak of the meaning of a thing by referring to something outside it. It may be thought that it provides, in fact, an illuminating parallel to the case of speaking about 'the meaning of life'.

My fear that it cannot be thought of in this way arises from its vociferous begging of the question. If we find unproblematical Wisdom's point that you can discuss the meaning of a play by talking about its 'internal relations', so to speak, this is surely only because a play has an author. As soon as we take a *natural* object – a landscape, say – and propose to discuss *its* meaning in the same way, the intelligibility of such a project is likely to fall under immediate challenge: to discuss a landscape's 'meaning' is to treat it as a work of art; to treat it as a work of art is to treat it as the work of an artist, and this is invalid – so the argument would be developed, and we should be back with the very question the would-be play parallel was thought of as illuminating.

Lest it be supposed that the supernaturalist has no analogous problems to those of the sceptic in this connection it may be worth pointing out that believing in a larger reality allows one to think of this one as having a meaning or point only at the expense of generating an unanswerable question just one step further back. For we can always try to ask: What is the meaning of this larger reality itself? And unless we are prepared to go on postulating larger and larger realities, *ad infinitum*, we must in the end have a question which demands the impossible: the placing of a reality in the context of a wider reality, when there is no such wider reality in which it can be placed. If we say that the meaning of this life lies in its relation to the life hereafter, the further question can be raised: and what is the meaning of this life and the after-life *taken as a whole*? – what is the meaning of the whole of existence in this new sense? It is clear that we thus begin an infinite regress. (See Wisdom, 'The Meanings of the Questions of Life', p. 40.) This does not necessarily rob the supernaturalist's account of the meaning of life of its significance. Similar regresses occur, for example, in explanation – regresses which the child exploits when he learns the trick of turning each successive *explicans* into a new *explicandum* – without vitiating the project of explaining alto-

72

gether. But it does show that it cannot be represented as a point in supernaturalism's favour that it has an answer to our question: What is the meaning of it all? whereas the secular man has none. This question cannot be answered except by generating a wider one of which the same is true.

There are some thinkers, of course, whose bafflement at answering these large questions from within a secular framework takes on a more belligerent tone than our own. They believe that this world is the only one, and that it 'has no meaning': but they go on to express this by saying that existence is 'absurd'.

This notion figures prominently in writers like Sartre and Camus, who constitute so important a part of the movement known (perhaps too vaguely) as Existentialism, and it seems to me worthwhile therefore to comment on it, particularly since it is a notion with more than a suspicion of paradox about it.

The air of paradox arises in the following way. The existentialist seems to be wanting on the one hand to say that existence has no meaning (in the sense that nothing lies beyond it) and yet on the other to attribute a certain kind of meaning to it, viz. absurdity. If it makes no sense, that is to say, to speak of 'the meaning of all things' it is surely just as wrong to say that existence is absurd unless *it makes sense* (although it would be false) to call it reasonable, intelligent, rational. An absurd remark is one that could have been penetrating; an absurd act is one that could have been inspired; an absurd suggestion might have been intelligent; an absurd idea might have been a bright one.

The point may be put in terms of a distinction Baier draws in the lecture already referred to, 'The Meaning of Life'. To call a thing meaningless, he points out, is sometimes a criticism, but sometimes not. 'There are many things that a man may do', he says, 'such as buying and selling, hiring labourers, ploughing, felling trees, and the like, which it is foolish, pointless, silly, perhaps crazy, to do if one has no purpose in doing them' (Baier, p. 19). To say a man was doing any of these things meaninglessly or purposelessly would thus be to criticise his behaviour. On the other hand, 'a row of trees growing near a farm may or may not have a purpose: it may or may not be a windbreak, may or may not have been planted or deliberately left standing there in order to prevent the wind from sweeping across the fields. . . . [But] we do not in any way disparage the trees if we say they have no purpose . . .' (Baier, p. 20). In this case, to call the trees meaningless or purposeless is not to level a criticism at all.

What the existentialist seems to be doing is to mix up these two things. He seems to be urging that existence lacks meaning in this second sense, and yet trying by the use of the term 'absurd' to represent this as a criticism.

Philip Thody, in his excellent book 'Albert Camus, 1913–60', puts what is essentially our point like this: 'In itself, the world can be neither absurd nor reasonable (in the secular man's view), since it is only man's mind which introduces the concept of reason by which, since it does not conform to it, the world can be judged absurd.'

But Thody goes on to explain how the paradox arises. In calling existence absurd the existentialist is talking in a compressed way partly about man's *reaction* to existence when he discovers the latter to lack meaning. It seems to him then to be absurd because he came to it with high expectations. He was hoping, had been deluded into thinking, that existence was meaningful and, moreover, rational. In the moment of disillusion he condemns existence as absurd, for it seems at that moment to embody the very reverse of the rationality he had been led to expect. Thody writes: 'The absurd can occur only when two elements are present – the desire of the human mind that the world should be explicable in human terms and the fact that the world is not thus explicable. "What is absurd," writes Camus, "is the clash between its irrationality and the desperate hunger for clarity which cries out in man's deepest soul" ' (Thody, p. 51).

The paradoxical notion of existence being both meaningless and absurd is therefore less puzzling than at first sight it may seem.

(c) *The meaning of an individual's life*
There is a closely related question of meaning to which we must now turn. So far we have been considering the issue of the meaning of life in general, the meaning of 'all this'. The related question arises however when an individual asks about the meaning not of life in general but of his *own* life. How is this

question about an individual life affected by the demise of 'the Supernatural'?

Again, more than one interpretation of the question is possible.

It is possible, first, to ask in this formula a question analogous to the second of those we discussed in relation to the whole of life: can life – now my individual life – be related to a wider context? Can it be seen as a part belonging to a whole?

Now that this question is being asked of an individual life, it is clear rather than problematical that rejecting 'the Supernatural' does not altogether rule out the possibility of one's life having this kind of meaning. For instead of seeing his earthly life as, say, a prelude to the life eternal, a man may see his life as playing a role within a purely secular project: he may for example devote himself to a secular cause – the abolition of slavery, the conservation of wild life, the spread of Communism. These are examples of projects which can be seen as more important than a single man's life, and which constitute wholes of which an individual life can be a part and from which an individual life may gain its meaning.

Suppose, however, that a man who has already rejected the notion of a 'supernatural' context for his life also refuses to dedicate himself to a secular cause of the kind we have mentioned. Are there circumstances in which it would be proper to say that *his* life had meaning? That is, is there another sense of a life's 'having meaning', which does not involve reference to a context outside that life?

There surely is. For often, when a man condemns his own life (for example) as 'meaningless' he means not only that he cannot see it as belonging to a greater whole, but that the activities that go to make it up have none of them any intrinsic worth. None of the things he does, he realises, are at all worth doing, and his life is thus revealed as a waste of time.

That there must be activities which are intrinsically worthwhile, which derive their value from nothing beyond themselves but which are valuable nonetheless, Wisdom reminds us with characteristic elegance in some words quoted by Ilham Dilman in his article 'Life and Meaning'. Wisdom makes the point with his favourite example of horse-racing:

Behind the words, 'What is the *purpose* of racing?' lies the innuendo that if it doesn't serve a purpose it is no good and waste of time [sic] and absurd. But the innuendo is itself absurd. For those things, such as surgical operations, or hewing coal, or what you will, which do serve a purpose, do so only because they are means to things which are worthwhile in themselves, worthwhile not because of any purpose they serve but because of what is in them – health and well-being before a warm fire, playing with a friend a game of draughts or ludo, if you like. (Wisdom, 'What is there in Horse Racing?', p. 1016)

It is perfectly proper, then, to speak of activities as worthwhile 'in themselves'; and it would certainly seem that the possibility of a man's life being meaningful or worthwhile in this sense is quite unaffected by whether he believes in a 'transcendent' reality.

The all-important question of what activities *are* worth pursuing for their own sakes, of what kind of life *is* intrinsically worthwhile we must leave on one side as strictly irrelevant to our discussion. (Ilham Dilman has interesting things to say about it in the article I have already mentioned.)

That this kind of 'intrinsic' meaningfulness is the only kind which we in these times can think of our lives as possessing is eloquently argued by Albert Camus in his essay 'Le mythe de Sisyphe' (and elsewhere). Sisyphus, as is well known, is condemned to spend eternity repeatedly pushing a large boulder to the top of a hill, on reaching which it falls to the bottom and has to be raised once more – and so on, *ad infinitum*. Here there is nothing beyond the raising of the boulder itself to give the enterprise meaning: the whole business seems utterly futile.

Nevertheless, Camus makes of Sisyphus a hero. For in spite of the fact that it can derive no meaning from without, the act is made to yield a meaning from within. Sisyphus derives enjoyment from the physical effort itself. His act becomes for him intrinsically worthwhile. In spite of everything, life is still to be loved and death despised: '. . . each of the specks on the stone, each glint of light on the surface of this mountain shrouded in night, is a universe in itself.' The realisation that this existence is the only existence, so far from excluding all meaning from life, for Camus rather reveals life's true meaning: 'A world remains in which man is the only master', or as he puts elsewhere, 'the fight towards the summit is itself sufficient to satisfy the heart of man' (Camus, quoted by Thody, pp. 53–4).

Does the loss of 'the Supernatural' rob life of its meaning? – that is the question we have been trying to answer. We have argued that construed as a question about an individual life, and about its being intrinsically worthwhile, there can be just as much 'meaning' with or without 'the Supernatural'. An individual life may, in another sense, equally well be said to have meaning (or 'point') in virtue of its belonging to a greater whole whether that whole is 'transcendent' or purely secular. But where we ask about the meaning of life or existence as a whole – 'What is the meaning of all this?' – I think the tenor of our argument was that we can only be clearly understood if a 'supernatural' or 'transcendent' framework is presupposed.

T. S. Eliot has written that a people without a 'supernatural' religion 'will in the end find that it has nothing to live for' ('A Conversation'). But do without a 'supernatural' religion we must, for the sufficient reason that we can no longer give a full and coherent sense to that notion: so I have argued. But I have also argued that this is not quite the disaster Eliot's words would lead us to expect. Secularisation involves changes, huge changes, in our way of regarding ourselves and our world, and adjusting to them may well be traumatic. But traumatic experiences are not always mortal, and sometimes, indeed, healthy development cannot proceed without them. I have tried to suggest that the loss of the 'supernatural' world by no means entails the loss of everything that we hold to be valuable. With Matthew Arnold, we too have heard the 'long, withdrawing roar' of secularisation:

> The sea of faith
> Was once, too, at the full, and round earth's shore
> Lay like the folds of a bright girdle furl'd;
> But now I only hear
> Its melancholy, long, withdrawing roar,
> Retreating to the breath
> Of the night-wind down the vast edges drear
> And naked shingles of the world.

The sound is a disturbing one, certainly; but to our ears not quite so melancholy.

Bibliography

I have asterisked works that may be generally helpful in pursuing the subject of this essay along a broad front. Where entries refer to works not mentioned in the text I have added a word of explanation.

W. P. Alston, 'Philosophy of Language' (Prentice-Hall, Englewood Cliffs, N.J., 1964).

T. J. J. Altizer and W. Hamilton, 'Radical Theology and The Death of God' (1966; Penguin Books ed., Harmondsworth, 1968).

S. S. Aquaviva, 'the Psychology of Dechristianisation in The Dynamics of the Industrial Society', in 'Social Compass', vii (1960). An interesting contribution, but difficult to get hold of.

M. Arnold, 'Dover Beach', numerous editions.

A. J. Ayer, 'Language, Truth and Logic' (1936; 2nd ed., Gollancz, London, 1946).

K. E. M. Baier, 'The Meaning of Life' (University College of Canberra, 1957).

P. L. Berger, 'The Social Reality of Religion' (1967, under the title 'The Sacred Canopy'; English ed., Faber & Faber, London, 1969). Very interesting and relevant but available too recently to be treated properly here.

H. J. Blackham, 'Religion in a Modern Society' (Constable, London, 1966). Relevant; some may find it interesting.

H. Blamires, 'The Christian Mind' (S.P.C.K., London, 1963).

D. Bohm, 'Causality and Chance in Modern Physics' (Routledge & Kegan Paul, London, 1957).

R. B. Braithwaite, 'An Empiricist's View of the Nature of Religious Belief', available in J. Hick (ed.), 'The Existence of God', q.v.

K. Britton, 'Philosophy and the Meaning of Life' Cambridge University Press, 1969). Too recently to hand to be discussed.

79

C. D. Broad, [1] 'Religion, Philosophy and Psychical Research' (Routledge & Kegan Paul, London, 1953).

C. D. Broad, [2] 'Lectures on Psychical Research' (Routledge & Kegan Paul, London, 1962).

P. van Buren, 'The Secular Meaning of the Gospel (S.C.M. Press, London, 1963).

A. Camus, 'Le Mythe de Sisyphe (Essai sur l'absurde) (Gallimard, 1943). English translation by Justin O'Brien, 'The Myth of Sisyphus' (Hamish Hamilton, London, 1955).

*H. Cox, 'The Secular City' (1965; S.C.M. cheap ed., London, 1966).

I. Dilman, 'Life and Meaning', in 'Philosophy', xl (1965).

P. Edwards, 'Meaning and Value of Life', in P. Edwards, 'The Encyclopædia of Philosophy (Macmillan and Free Press, New York, etc., 1967). A helpful introduction.

T.S. Eliot, 'A Conversation', in 'The Listener', lxxxii (11 Sept 1969) 2111. The source of the quotation which heads Chapter 2.

J. Epstein, 'Epstein, an Autobiography' (1955; 2nd ed., Studio Vista, London, 1963).

E. E. Evans-Pritchard, see E. E. E. Pritchard.

F. Ferré, 'Language, Logic and God' (Eyre & Spottiswoode, London, 1962). A valuable discussion of many topics in our Chapter 2.

A. G. N. Flew, [1] 'Hume's Philosophy of Belief' (Routledge & Kegan Paul, London, 1961).

A. G. N. Flew, [2] 'Theology and Falsification (a contribution to a discussion)', in A. G. N. Flew and A. MacIntyre, 'New Essays in Philosophical Theology, q.v.

A. G. N. Flew and A. MacIntyre, (eds.), 'New Essays in Philosophical Theology' (S.C.M. Press, London, 1955).

J. Galsworthy, 'A Modern Comedy' (Heinemann, London, 1929).

P. Geach, 'God and the Soul' (Routledge & Kegan Paul, London, 1969).

J. Glanvill, 'Sadducismus Triumphatus' (1668 (but see the reference to Willey in my text, p. 10 above); 3rd ed., London,1689).

G. Gorer, 'Exploring English Character' (Cresset Press, London, 1955).

J. Gould, (ed.), 'Penguin Survey of the Social Sciences, 1965, (Penguin Books, Harmondsworth, 1965).
80

K. Grahame, 'The Wind in the Willows' (Methuen, London, 1908).

R. W. Hepburn, 'Christianity and Paradox' (Watts, London, 1958).

J. Hick, (ed.), [1] 'Faith and the Philosophers' (Macmillan, London, 1964).

J. Hick, (ed.), [2] 'The Existence of God' (Macmillan, New York, etc., 1964).

R. Hoggart, 'The Uses of Literacy' (Chatto & Windus, London, 1957).

W. Howitt, 'The History of the Supernatural' (London, 1863).

W. D. Hudson, 'On two points against Wittgensteinian Fideism', in 'Philosophy', xliii (July 1968). A reply to K. Nielsen, 'Wittgensteinian Fideism', q.v.

W. James, 'The Varieties of Religous Experience' (Longmans, Green, London, 1945).

R. F. Jones, 'The Seventeenth Century' (Stanford University Press, Stanford and London, 1951).

M. Laski, 'Ecstasy – A study of some Secular and Religious Experiences' (Cresset Press, London, 1961). For those who want to look further at the possibility of secular experience analogous to experience of the 'numinous'.

*W. E. H. Lecky, 'History of the Rise and Influence of Rationalism in Europe (1865; cheaper ed., reprinted, Longmans, Green, London, 1913).

C. S. Lewis, 'The Discarded Image' Cambridge University Press, 1964). A fascinating account of the medieval worldview.

*A. MacIntyre, [1] 'Secularisation and Moral Change' (Oxford University Press, 1967).

A. MacIntyre, [2] 'Is Understanding Religion compatible with Believing?', in J. Hick (ed.), 'Faith and the Philosophers, q.v.

A. MacIntyre and A. G. N. Flew, 'New Essays in Philosophical Theology' see under A. G. N. Flew and A. MacIntyre.

D. Martin, [1] 'Towards Eliminating the Concept of Secularization', now available as the first chapter of D. Martin, 'The Religious and the Secular, q.v.

*D. Martin, [2] 'The Religious and the Secular' (Routledge & Kegan Paul, London, 1969).

*E. L. Mascall, [1] 'The Secularization of Christianity' (Darton, Longman & Todd, London, 1965).

E. L. Mascall, [2] 'Words and Images' (Longmans, Green, London, etc., 1957).

B. E. Meland, 'The Secularization of Modern Cultures (Oxford University Press, New York, 1966). A speculative analysis of modern societies with particular reference to India.

J. S. Mill, [1] 'On Liberty', reprinted in M. Warnock, (ed.), 'Utilitarianism,' q.v.

J. S. Mill, [2] 'System of Logic' (London, 1843).

B. Mitchell, (ed.), 'Faith and Logic' (Allen & Unwin, London, 1957). A useful collection of philosophico-theological essays, mostly relating to our Chapter 2.

J. W. Montgomery, 'A Philosophical-Theological Critique of the Death of God Movement', in B. Murchland, (ed.), 'The Meaning of the Death of God', q.v.

B. Murchland, (ed.), 'The Meaning of the Death of God' (Random House, New York, 1967).

F. W. H. Myers, E. Gurney and F. Podmore, 'Phantasms of the Living' (London, 1886).

E. Nagel, 'The Structure of Science' (Routledge & Kegan Paul, London, 1961).

K. Nielsen, [1] 'Wittgensteinian Fideism', in 'Philosophy', xlii (July 1967).

K. Nielsen, [2] 'Wittgensteinian Fideism: A Reply to Hudson', in 'Philosophy', xliv (Jan 1969). What it says – see W. D. Hudson, 'On two points against Wittgensteinian Fideism', q.v.

R. Otto, 'The Idea of the Holy', Trans. J. W. Harvey (1917; Pelican ed., Penguin Books, Harmondsworth, 1959).

D. A. Pailin, 'Christian and Atheist', in 'London Quarterly and Holborn Review' (Oct. 1967). A review of the Death of God movement.

W. and L. Pelz, 'God is No More' (1963; 3rd impression, Gollancz, London, 1964).

D. Z. Phillips, [1] 'Religion and Understanding' (Blackwell, Oxford, 1967).

D. Z. Phillips, [2] 'Wisdom's Gods', in *Philosophical Quarterly*, xix (Jan 1969).

D. Z. Phillips, [3] 'The Concept of Prayer' (Routledge & Kegan Paul, London, 1965).

F. Podmore, 'The Naturalisation of the Supernatural' (Putnam, New York and London, 1908). I borrowed this title for the heading of section 1.2.(*a*).

E. E. E. Pritchard, 'Witchcraft Oracles and Magic among the Azande' (Clarendon Press, Oxford, 1937).

W. V. O. Quine, 'Two Dogmas of Empiricism', in the same author's 'From a Logical Point of View' (1953; 2nd ed., Harvard University Press, Cambridge, Mass., 1961).

I. T. Ramsey, 'Religious Language' (1957; paperback ed., Macmillan, New York, 1963).

J. A. T. Robinson, 'Honest to God' (S.C.M. Press, London, 1963).

L. J. Russell, 'The Meaning of Life', in *Philosophy*, xxviii (1953). A helpful discussion.

J. Searle, 'Speech Acts' (Cambridge University Press, 1969).

M. A. Simon, 'When is a Resemblance a Family Resemblance?', in *Mind*, lxxviii (July 1969).

C. Smith, 'Contemporary French Philosophy' (Methuen, London, 1964). May be helpful in connection with 'the absurd'.

N. K. Smith, 'Is Divine Existence Credible?', in D. Z. Phillips (ed.), 'Religion and Understanding', q.v.

R. G. Smith, 'Secular Christianity' (Collins, London, 1966). A relevant study belonging to a tradition other than that of the present essay.

J. R. Smythies (ed.), 'Science and E.S.P.' (Routledge & Kegan Paul, London, 1967).

W. T. Stace, 'Mysticism and Philosophy' (Macmillan, London, 1961).

P. Thody, 'Albert Camus, 1913–60' (1961; paperback ed., Hamish Hamilton, London, 1964).

P. van Buren, see under Buren.

A. R. Vidler (ed.), 'Soundings' (Cambridge University Press, 1962). 'Progressive' theologians discuss Christianity's shape and role in the contemporary world.

M. Warnock (ed.), 'Utilitarianism' (Fontana ed., Collins, London, 1962).

W. Whewell, 'The Philosophy of the Inductive Sciences' (1840; facsimile of the 2nd ed. (London, 1847), Johnson Reprint Corporation, New York and London, 1967).

B. Willey, [1] 'The Touch of Cold Philosophy', in R. F. Jones (ed.), 'The Seventeenth Century', q.v.

B. Willey, [2] 'The Seventeenth Century Background' (Chatto & Windus, London, 1934).

*B. Wilson, 'Religion in Secular Society' (1966; Pelican ed., Penguin Books, Harmondsworth, 1969).

P. Winch, [1] 'The Idea of a Social Science' (Routledge & Kegan Paul, London, 1958).

P. Winch, [2] 'Understanding a Primitive Society', now available in D. Z. Phillips, 'Religion and Understanding, q.v.

J. Wisdom, [1] 'Gods', in J. Wisdom, 'Philosophy and Psychoanalysis, q.v.

J. Wisdom, [2] 'Philosophy and Psychoanalysis' (1953; 4th impression, Blackwell, Oxford, 1969).

J. Wisdom, [3] 'Religious Belief', in J. Wisdom, 'Paradox and Discovery', q.v.

J. Wisdom, [4] 'Paradox and Discovery' (Blackwell, Oxford, 1965).

J. Wisdom, [5] 'The Logic of God', in J. Wisdom, 'Paradox and Discovery, q.v.

J. Wisdom, [6] 'Other Minds' (Blackwell, Oxford, 1965).

J. Wisdom, [7] 'The Meanings of the Questions of Life', in J. Wisdom, 'Paradox and Discovery', q.v.

J. Wisdom, [8] 'What is there in Horse Racing?', in 'The Listener' (10 June 1954).

L. Wittgenstein, 'Philosophical Investigations' (1953; 2nd ed., English text reprint, Blackwell, Oxford, 1963).

G. F. Wood, 'The Idea of the Transcendent', in A. R. Vidler (ed.), 'Soundings', q.v. Some have found this helpful (though I am not among them).

R. C. Zaehner, 'Mysticism, sacred and profane' (1957; paperback ed., Oxford University Press, 1961). More about the possibility of 'secular' mystical experience.